JOURS of OUR LIVES

JOURS OF
OUR LIVES

On The Road In France
and Beyond

BETH ARNOLD

Alastair & Arnold

Illustrations by Elizabeth Cannon,
http://elizabethcannoncouture.net

Printed in the United States of America

ISBN: 978-1-7339364-0-8 (eBook)

978-1-7339364-1-5 (Paperback)

For my wonderful daughters, Blair and Bret, who bravely went with us on our journey to France, whether they wanted to or not. They have grown into amazing women, magnificent human beings. I couldn't be prouder of them.

CONTENTS

Prologue // *"Pardon Me, But You Are a Dreamer"* ix

Chapter One // *The Bumpy Landing* 1

Chapter Two // *Nomads with Luggage* 4

Chapter Three // *Technology May Kill Us* 7

Chapter Four // *Settling In* 10

Chapter Five // *Auntie Mame* 13

Chapter Six // *Ghosts of Christmas Past* 16

Chapter Seven // *A Light in the Window* 21

Chapter Eight // *Here Comes The Sun* 25

Chapter Nine // *Northern Exposure* 29

Chapter Ten // *Each Step I Take* 32

Chapter Eleven // *When It Feels So Right* 35

Chapter Twelve // *The Spirits of Belle Ile* 39

Chapter Thirteen // *The Island Lure* 43

Chapter Fourteen // *The Borrowed Home* 46

Chapter Fifteen // *A Part of Something* 49

Chapter Sixteen // *Letting Go* 52

Chapter Seventeen // *The Enchanted Weekend* 56

Chapter Eighteen // *The Light of The South* 60

Chapter Nineteen // *The Healing Land* 65

Chapter Twenty // *Coup de Foudre* 69

Chapter Twenty-One // *As Dreamers Do* 73

Chapter Twenty-Two // *Blow The House Down* 77

Chapter Twenty-Three // *Abandonment* 81

Chapter Twenty-Four // *Shedding My Skin* 85

Chapter Twenty-Five // *The View From On High* 89

Chapter Twenty-Six // *Lily of the Valley* 93

Chapter Twenty-Seven // *House of Dreams* 97

Chapter Twenty-Eight // *Days of Heaven* 101

Chapter Twenty-Nine // *A Little Piece of St. Tropez* 106

Chapter Thirty // *The Last Supper* 110

Chapter Thirty-One // *Life in Collioure* 113

Chapter Thirty-Two // *My Circling Theory* 117

Chapter Thirty-Three // *Riders of The Storm* 121

Chapter Thirty-Four // *Called By Color* 125

Chapter Thirty-Five // *Woven Voices* 129

Chapter Thirty-Six // *On The Road* 133

Chapter Thirty-Seven // *The Port of Tangier* 137

Chapter Thirty-Eight // *Mission Accomplished* 141

Chapter Thirty-Nine // *Kicked Out...To Paris* 145

Epilogue 149

Acknowledgments 151

About Beth Arnold 155

PROLOGUE

"Pardon Me, But You Are a Dreamer"

M Y HUSBAND AND I sat in a small, cramped real estate office on a busy street in Collioure, France. We had come here in pursuit of artist Henri Matisse, whose life and art we were researching, and who had spent so many summers painting in Collioure. Our plan was to spend a chunk of time here, soaking up the charm of this former fishing village and its surrounding cork oak woodlands and cascading vineyards, with the Mediterranean lapping at its Eastern shores and the snow-capped Pyrenees Mountains anchoring the Western horizon. We were bewitched by Collioure's beauty.

What my husband—Jim Morgan—and I were discovering as we followed in Matisse's footsteps around France was that Monsieur Matisse and great artists like him find the most beautiful places to live and work, and these geographical entities have a distinctive, open, and creative vibe. You know the kinds of settings I mean. In the United States, these are towns like Santa Fe and Taos, New Mexico; Blowing Rock, North Carolina; Ocean Springs, Mississippi; Berea, Kentucky; and Woodstock, New York. People feel *good* there.

For artists, light is a key to how they see the world around them. In the early years of the 20th Century, the pink light of Collioure illuminated the spirits of Matisse, Andre Derain, Raoul Dufy, Maurice de Vlaminck, Kees von Dongen, Georges Braque, and other artists, who had come to ignite their canvasses with saturated colors and loose brushwork. The French art world was horrified by this shocking breach of un-sanctioned creativity. A critic dubbed these rebel artists *les Fauves*—the wild beasts—for their audaciousness.

Jim and I felt a bit like wild beasts ourselves. We were on our own passage that would change our lives remarkably—a breathtakingly grand adventure that was fulfilling a dream I'd had since I was 19 years old, on my first trip to Europe: to actually *live* there.

* * *

IT HAD BEEN anything but easy. This whole crazy journey started one day in 2001, when Jim asked for my help with a new book idea. I am literally his muse—what we now call a creative—and in those days Jim and I spent a lot of time talking about potential projects, concepts for movies or books, even Broadway musicals. It was one of our areas of common ground that fed our relationship.

One thing I know is this: The heart is where the ideas are. People react first with emotion and make decisions from emotion. Emotion is exactly where artists grab their readers or audience. Give an audience a scene or situation they can latch onto, and they're in for the story, no matter what form it takes.

I had read an article in the Writers Guild West magazine called "Entertaining The Issues," which basically said that if you have a message to get across, don't bombard your audience with dry facts and information—no one will listen or finish reading. Instead, tell them a story. "Entertain" the issues so that your audience gets hooked emotionally and wants to go along for the ride.

We sometimes use *heart* or *gut* interchangeably to describe the centers in which we feel emotion. And intuition—the ability to understand something immediately, without the need for conscious reasoning—stirs in us as well. It comes to us as whispers, or feelings that we can learn to pay attention to. There have been many people in my life who've wanted to discount my feelings/emotions/intuition. "You're not being rational," they would say.

Well, how about this: Psychologists Amos Tversky and Daniel Kahneman launched the field of Behavioral Economics, which showed that man *is* a very irrational being—and that feeling is basically a form of thinking. What I know is that when I'm coming up with ideas or being creative, I'm tapping into my authentic self. I believe this is true for most people. We're all creators—this is part of our spiritual job here on Earth. Whether we're creating the lives we want to live, or cooking up a new recipe, or organizing our mounds of stuff, or starting a business, we create in almost everything we do. It makes us feel alive—connected to ourselves and to the Universe.

So on this day in 2001, Jim and I were kicking ideas around. I was thinking about who he is and what he loves. Besides being a writer, Jim is also a painter. He loves art—we both do. He had recently fallen in love with Matisse's *Jazz* book, the wonderful collection of the artist's cutouts. Matisse had created these collages late in life, when he could no longer paint or sculpt. But he was still driven to express himself and his creativity—to live his life.

We never know how the people we meet and the places we go may show up in future synchronicities. My late brother, Brent Arnold, was a decorator in New York whom David Halberstam called "the talent of his generation." In 1989, when Jim and I married and moved into our Craftsman house in Little Rock, Brent gave us a short but brilliant piece of advice on decorating our new home: "Matisse colors and Vuillard patterns." We immediately got it: We loved Matisse's bright colors, and Édouard Vuillard's rich texture of fabric on fabric was just perfect for us.

Brent's advice was Jim's initial impetus to start digging into Matisse, and over the ensuing decade he had become a true admirer of the painter. He had even started painting again himself, after having put it aside for decades. So when it came to finding the right idea for Jim's book, I knew that painting in general and Matisse in particular felt genuine to him in a strong and intoxicating way.

The book concept I came up with was called "Learning to See." Most people go through their lives just looking, and not really seeing. Real artists *see*. If you're going to be an artist, you have to train yourself to *see*. So through Matisse, Jim would explore what actual "seeing" meant. What do we find when we delve beneath the surface, when we comprehend on a deeper level? What had Matisse taught us with his life and art? What did Matisse and his life and art mean to Jim and me at what would become a pivotal juncture in our lives?

Jim sold his book proposal to Simon & Schuster's Free Press imprint, though the idea shifted slightly and the title changed to *Chasing Matisse*. Jim and I were thrilled. We had been feeling an unrelenting pull to make a big change—a change of energy and scenery. We didn't know how long we would be in France chasing Matisse, and the general plan was to move to the Hudson Valley once this adventure was over. But I had wanted my children to live abroad as a defining experience of their childhoods, and time had slipped away. I'd never made it happen. As a family, we had spent six amazing weeks in France in the summer of 1998. That experience had changed all of us, and I had been waiting to find a way to live there before more time escaped. For as long as we were in France, Blair and Bret could come as often as possible.

That was the upside. The reality is that dismantling a life isn't easy. The immensity of making this expedition happen didn't hit us all at once, which was probably the only way we could deal with everything we had to do. It took us months and months to be ready to leave. For one thing, our younger daughter, Bret, needed to complete her senior year in high school, which she would do in May 2002. For another, there was the house we all loved, the place where our blended family had come together and become whole.

Our house was lovely, comfortable, well located, and sort of famous— Jim had written a book about it called *If These Walls Had Ears: The Biography of A House*. The house was our treasure, our grand statement that visually showed who we were individually, as a couple, as a family. We'd spent a crazy amount of time wandering through antique stores and flea markets, finding just the right lamps, tables, and fabrics. Much of Brent's stylish furniture was there—blue leather recamiers, a three-quarter bed with a leopard needlepoint headboard outlined with brass upholstery tacks, a table in the shape of a cannon, a black lacquer cloverleaf bar, a lovely silk pouf that Brent had designed but never saw finished. He died before it was done. I could go on and on. People came into our space and were wowed by it. And just like that, we were letting it go.

Our beautiful house was photographed twice for magazines. The second shoot was during this period of preparing to move. One of the setups was of the four of us standing on the front porch with our schnauzer, Snapp. Bret didn't want to do the shoot. She hated for us to sell the house, and she'd sobbed so much that she had to wear sunglasses for the photo. We all slipped on our shades in solidarity.

That fall, we drove Bret to Hollins University in Roanoke, Virginia, for college. She would be exploring a different part of the country, making new friends, getting a grip on college life, understanding her life in a different way.

We later learned that even though Bret was excited to go off to college, when Jim and I actually left for France she felt like we had abandoned her. This realization was heartbreaking, and I beat myself up because I hadn't intuited that this was likely to happen. If I could zip back in time for a re-do, I would let her finish her freshman year before we left. But, as you'll see, there were other traumatic events yet to come.

Bret's older sister, Blair, somehow decided that since we were leaving, it was time to get married. I don't think it was a *conscious* connection—it was more subtle than that. Blair and her boyfriend announced their engagement and started vaguely thinking about a wedding. A few months later, Jim and I with some friends threw a small engagement party. But before the nuptials even got close to being definite, the couple broke up. That was a relief to everybody.

Meanwhile, we spent months gradually boxing up our house for a future move across country—though first the boxes were going to storage until we returned from France. Some of our best friends supported us by helping us pack. Can you imagine such a gift?

We were finally ready to leave in November 2002, or at least as ready as we could be. We'd bought our tickets to Paris and packed suitcases and boxes to ship. The plan was to stay in Paris long enough to get set up and settled. We'd spend Christmas there, and the girls would join us, before we took off in our leased station wagon in which all of our belongings would be packed, including office supplies, files, a printer, and a framed print of Frida Kahlo from an exhibition at the Maillol Museum in Paris that our family had loved on a previous trip. Frida wanted to come along, and I was happy for her to join us.

The day before Thanksgiving, we drove Bret's cat, Cleo, and our dog, Snapp, to Batesville, where my mother lived. She had agreed to keep them. We spent a difficult night with her. She was so sad that we were leaving. She understood what we were doing and why, but I think she felt that we were abandoning her, too. On Thanksgiving Day itself, we didn't even stay for the holiday meal. We left my mother in her driveway, crying. I was sobbing, too. How could I know that I would never see her again?

* * *

IN PLANNING OUR great adventure, Jim and I had needed to find a way to defray the enormous cost of traveling through France. The basic idea was to build a website, chronicle our journey as it was happening, and trade unbooked hotel rooms for a plug on our website. I was to build the content as we sojourned from one Matisse domain to the next. This was *before* the Digital Revolution—before we even knew about Google—but somehow I intuitively felt this seismic shift coming. Our web guy said, "Beth, you're going to write something called a Weblog, and you're going to buy a digital camera and take pictures for it." Nobody, including me, even knew what a Weblog—or blog—was, but I said okay.

Besides the blog, I was writing Travel Recommendations about hotels, restaurants, anything that grabbed my fancy or gave me joy. I felt that this was a real opportunity for these hotels, restaurants, car leasing outfits, anybody we could think of, to start an online presence, to be listed in my guide and/or in my blog. Today this notion seems nothing but run-of-the-mill. But who was doing that in those days?

I am an INFP on the Meyers-Briggs test, which means Introverted-Intuitive-Feeling-Perceiving, and even though I believed in our project with all my heart, I had to steel myself to walk into a strange place, ask people I didn't know—whose language I was massacring—to *give* us a room for several nights. It's experiences like these that build you up or tear you down. Some of the hoteliers got it, loved what we were doing, and were happy to participate. Others didn't.

The publisher was absolutely clueless about what a blog would or could do for them and the book—how it would set them up to enter the Digital Age and how they could begin learning how to use this extraordinary global resource. The company refused to support our site financially, so we paid for it all ourselves. Design is extremely important to me, and we were determined to do it right. Building and maintaining the site was very, very expensive. We worked hard to minimize expenses the whole trip.

Which brings me back to the beginning—Jim and me sitting in the tiny real estate office in Collioure. I was explaining to the Madame that we would like to propose coverage on our website for a stay in a particular property that had a stunning view of Collioure and the Mediterranean. The owners weren't there. It wasn't rented. I gave her my pitch, which I had honed well by this time. I hoped she would have vision, I said.

She didn't. She wouldn't even propose it to them. "These people will want *money*!" she said. "Pardon me, Madame, but you are a dreamer."

Her words were like an arrow piercing my heart. It was true. I was guilty of being a dreamer. I had long been criticized by some members of my family with different words but with similar meaning—and so had Brent. We were the artistic ones. It hurt me then, but today I wear it like a medal on my virtual suit of armor. Yes, I am a dreamer, and I also have vision, *my* vision, which doesn't have to be like anyone else's. In fact it shouldn't be. I ride the cutting edge of the cultural wave with grace and authority. And I accept myself.

This book, *Jours of Our Lives,* was my blog for *Chasing Matisse,* as we traveled through France following Matisse's life path. This was the most exciting journey of *my* life, as well as one of the hardest. You know some of the reasons already, and others will reveal themselves to you as you read my pages. I went from knowing nothing about the digital world or writing a blog to becoming quite efficient and knowledgeable.

Every single day, I chanced on joy and delight. I learned about myself and pushed myself to new limits. I worked my butt off. I believe you'll see my growth in the pages you're about to read.

Our hopes and dreams were wrapped up in this adventure just as the hopes and dreams of *les Fauves* had been in theirs. My wish is that *Jours of Our Lives* will inspire you to take your own journey, whatever and wherever it happens to be.

Please find a way to believe in yourselves. Don't let anyone stop you. Good luck and Godspeed.

Sending love,

Beth

The real voyage of discovery consists not in seeking new landscapes, but in having new eyes.

—Marcel Proust

You can't connect the dots looking forward; you can only connect them looking backwards. So you have to trust that the dots will somehow connect in your future. You have to trust in something— your gut, destiny, life, karma, whatever. This approach has never let me down, and it has made all the difference in my life.

—Steve Jobs

CHAPTER ONE
The Bumpy Landing

IT STARTED WHEN we checked into the wrong hotel. We walked up the cobblestone street with our five huge pieces of luggage, me wearing my mother's luscious mink coat and feeling very grand. We stepped into what we thought was going to be a creamy lobby, a charming and beautiful hotel. Instead it was small, worn, and drab. The floor was being mopped, and it felt like with my hair. With our carry-ons, we barely fit into the elevator. On the second floor, we were shown to a tiny room with the walls the color of Arkansas pond scum and the wooden trim an enamel Kelly green. We thought we might have to sleep on our luggage piled on our beds as "The Princess and The Prince and The Very Uncomfortable Pea." I wanted to say, "Quel dommage!" although I'm not sure what it means. We ran out of time for our French lessons as we were sweating over all the details to leave. It has the right sound anyway.

We'd worked so hard to get here, leaving what was left undone. Then we, along with our adult daughters, Blair and Bret, and our dear friend Patti boo-hooed as we drove away. This of course required a stiff drink at the airport, though not another one until we boarded our Air France flight in Atlanta. When drinks were served, we had to have Champagne. We finally were on our way.

At Charles DeGaulle airport, we snagged a wonderful driver named Jacques who had a van that could hold all Our Stuff. We told him about *Chasing Matisse*, feeling very proud. He talked about Paris and delivered us to what we thought would be the haven for us to rest and sleep—to relax after this six-month-sprint to leave our old lives behind and learn to see in the new lives we would find.

Unfortunately, we thought we had booked the four-star Victoria Palace. We had arrived in Paris to begin our big adventure, but Jacques had delivered us to the address we told him—the Victoria Hotel. Definitely not the right one, though we still didn't get it. Our friend Mims had told us about how beautiful the Victoria Palace was. "Poor Mims," we said, looking around the Victoria Hotel. "Somebody sold him a bill of goods." As Jacques drove away and left us, it seemed absolutely appropriate that his last name was Misery.

We stayed in bed for 16 hours, and I'm not talking about a honeymoon. I mean hard-core not-even-snoring sleep, when Paris was waiting outside our window. But we couldn't have cared. My dreams were coming one after another and were intense, visions with me looking down on water—from a small, placid lake in lush countryside to flying with ethereal wings above a huge lake and not knowing how to get down until I hit a gentle waterfall and slid into the big pond. The most disturbing fantasy was Jim and me standing on a huge cliff looking down on a swirling, restless sea. Our son Matt was with us. A man walked up to the edge and stepped off. I knew Matt wanted to do the same and asked him not to, but he took the leap. Jim may have jumped too, and I don't know about me. But then I had an underwater view of them and others speeding around in a clear submarine navigating jauntily.

I went from Dreamland messages in my own head to actually trying to set up our French Internet connection. That was the real nightmare. After we finally woke up, we headed over to the Internet café around the corner. I could hardly think and my vision was blurry, still tired as could be. We spent two hours in the first foray and six hours more the next day. If one of our computers was up and running, the other wasn't, and then we still couldn't get email. This went on for days. Meals were sporadic. Our hotel room and the Internet café were all we saw.

We were wrung out...then it seemed part of our setup was working. We grabbed a bite of lunch at a Vietnamese kiosk close to the hotel and then went to buy a cell phone, so we could be communicado in that old-fashioned mode. In a matter of a half-hour, it was success! Not nearly as hard as dealing with our server—until we discovered we really needed to know the language to press the right buttons.

We sauntered back into our hotel. I waved and smiled at the tall thin man with glasses, who looked like a Rotweiler, standing at the desk. He snarled at me. "You owe 43 euros for the Internet, and you must pay it now." Okay. I mean what's the problem. We paid the snarly man and went up to our room. Then two boxes of books and supplies of Our Stuff arrived that had been shipped, and we knew we had to get out of there. No matter what, we had to leave.

Actually, it was minutes later that we discovered we'd checked into the wrong hotel. When we called Mims, he asked, "Are you at the Victoria Palace on the Left Bank?" The shock permeated our bones, horrible yet funny. We'd checked into the wrong hotel. How utterly imperfect.

But later that evening, as we tromped through Paris on a mission to find another place to stay, we found out we were saved! Mims had followed up on a letter I'd sent to Randall Vemer at French Home Rentals, and Randall had put him in touch with owner Michel Tessel. Michel liked our project, and he dashed in like a Musketeer! We had a free apartment in the Marais for three weeks!

CHAPTER TWO

Nomads with Luggage

THE NEXT MORNING we talked with Claire at French Home Rentals, who called someone named Ruben, who was to meet us at the apartment, 14 rue du Perche, just around the corner from the Picasso Museum. She also arranged a taxi that could carry all Our Stuff. I didn't remember so many Paris cabs being minivans, but there are quite a few—and so convenient! Claire's assistance was angelic, since we were half brain-dead and still recovering from the shock of what we'd done, although the humor didn't miss us. The snarly man was at the hotel desk when we left. I again was wearing Mother's mink coat and feeling grand to be leaving, much like the Queen of Sheba, while he would have to stay in the drab little place he called a hotel.

We are nomads in this new life of ours, which implies we shouldn't be carrying so many bags, unless we had a caravan. We don't have a fleet of camels or even a tiny car. Therein lies a basic conflict.

I often have this problem when I'm packing for a trip. I like to have my stuff along. At home, I dress for my mood du jour. I gaze into my closet and usually something calls to me—a shirt, a skirt, a pair of shoes—that looks exactly how I feel. I slip it on, and from there, the ensemble (or lack of one) comes together. But this wasn't an ordinary trip. This was moving, traveling for months. And it wasn't like days of old, when steamer trucks carried a lady's collection of clothing. You could check two bags on the airlines but paid dearly for any more. And we carried more than clothes. We were lugging computers, files, a

CHAPTER THREE
Technology May Kill Us

JIM'S LAPTOP JUST quit working. A blank screen was staring at us no matter what he did, and he simmered up a minor meltdown himself, though not as bad as it could've been—and not to the extent that I probably would've lost it with our technological setbacks and the stress that has generated. Our wits aren't wired industrially. Oh, maybe if we really tried they could be, but that would be excruciating too. The point is that attempting to get our European "theater of operations" up and working has eaten us alive.

The lone Parisian activity we've had any time for are long walks down the boulevards and rues, exploring our neighborhood while looking for just the right dinner setting. This is one of the great joys of Paris. We walked in Little Rock for fitness, not to travel from one place to another, nor as an enjoyable pursuit in and of itself, nor to find another architectural beauty or scene we hadn't laid eyes on before. We could have strolled and appreciated our own surroundings, even if they weren't Paris, but didn't. That was a decision we made in how we lived our lives. Growing up, our daughters wouldn't have considered walking four or five blocks to the video store. "I'd be embarrassed to be seen walking," our younger daughter once said. We do not see what we have. We're too busy driving by it.

There's also the matter of instant gratification, time and how we perceive it. How do we live with the concepts of speed and slowness? Milan Kundera, one of my favorite authors, addresses these ideas in his novel *Slowness*—how human beings think and feel, act and respond.

Time is a trickster, and it is part of our challenge here in Paris. We're being killed by the technology, but we must have the immediacy of the Internet for our communications network. And yet the most interesting point in this project for me—the learning to see—is all about slowness.

One afternoon after we'd been to the huge department store BHV (actual name Bazaar d'Hotel de Ville) to buy more electrical and business supplies, we met Ruben and Chloe at the trendy Le Fumoir to connect, buy them a drink, and apologize for having missed the Louvre party. Chloe, an American artist who has lived in Paris for more than 20 years, takes whatever job she must to make ends meet. Ruben is Argentine and has been here 12 years.

Chloe talked about what a tough city Paris is—but how great the quality of life. It's been my contention for years that artists are not supported in the U.S.—not financially, culturally, individually, or as a group. Art and the creating of art, which is a great equalizer and connector—the enjoyment of it is available to anyone in any class—is generally not valued. Respect for art forms, which enrich our spirits, life condition, and society, is dismissed. Ruben and Chloe discussed how hard it is to survive as an artist in Paris, but Chloe agreed that artists are better thought of here than at home.

Being here really is different this time. We're not tourists breaking our necks. We're working, trying to get set up and get organized. We haven't even made the pilgrimage to our favorite haunts on the Left Bank. The weird thing is we don't even care.

In the meantime, we couldn't work the phone that we were so proud to have. We could dial a number, but we couldn't retrieve messages or do other basic functions. We couldn't even hear the phone ring. We'd chosen the "polite" tone, which I then changed to "espionage." It startles me when I hear it.

After a maddening, draining, couldn't-make-anything-work day, we strolled down the rue des Archives on our evening ritual. Several shop windows entertained us with their displays of S & M accessories.

The boy crowd was spilling out of one of their favorite bars to hang outside, bald heads and hard bodies clad in leather pants and vests. They had an urban, polished/rough edge, or they could've been in a musical. I told Jim I might ask them how much they'd give me for him. Gay men always love Jim, which he should take as proof-positive that he's still got it. But that isn't enough for him. He still longs for hair, especially hair with color.

After that, we came home and burned up the printer. We're learning the hard way about French electricity and the gizmos we do or don't need to go with our machines. Important distinction: Adaptors are not the same as converters. And surge protectors don't help at all.

The good news was, we heard from Europe By Car about a model to lease when we get on the road, and that was exciting! All the choices were interesting—a little station wagon with a huge sun roof that opened to the sky, a large sedan with a GPS system, or a little van that could hold Our Stuff. Ooh, this is good!

At dinner, we saw two little dogs trot into our restaurant with their owners, which pleased us much and made us think of our Snapp at home with his grandmother. Somehow, by the end of the day, we'd made a leap. We felt like things were going to change and go more smoothly.

As Hemingway said, "Isn't it pretty to think so."

CHAPTER FOUR

Settling In

I'D READ IT, heard it countless times before, but I didn't get it. Everyone talked about how great the Marais was, and I thought what's the big deal? But now that we've been here two weeks, I'm in the know. We love the Marais! We love our Perche apartment and the building it's in—even though it took us a week to figure out how to turn on the lights in the hall at night whenever we needed to go downstairs. A neighbor finally showed us.

The streets around us have become familiar. We do most of our grocery shopping on the rue de Bretagne, at the supermarket with the $3 bottles of wine we like. The Jouannault Maitre Fromager, at No. 39, is where Jim whiffed the stinky smell of cheese. His "something sure stinks around here" line will haunt him forever, so it's perfect that this is where we buy our fromage. At No. 25 is La Fougasse, where I buy delicious brown cereal bread and little ficelles that are the perfect size for us. The shopkeeper there is a small dark-haired woman with heart-shaped lips. We've tasted her tartelettes of Provence, pizza, chevre, and Roquefort with mouth-watering success. There's something about a little round of pastry filled with savory ingredients that locks my eyes to them before my nose or tastebuds have even gotten a chance. I simply can't buy bread without also buying one of these miniature pies. On the other hand, I've shown great muscle by turning my back to the pastries and chocolates.

I needed to lose weight before I left home and just couldn't do it. Now each day I get up thinking I'll be thinner. Each morning, no luck. Oh, I might have lost a pound or two. I'm not really dieting, but I'm not eating many sweets. I'm semi-watching my cheese and fat intake though not cutting them out. Each night I have wine but not that much. I'm eating well, though not over-indulging. I hope this reasonable way of eating will work.

We've gotten to know the BHV very well. I have been busy as a little worker bee organizing Our Stuff into what I'm calling "modular units." It's not that there's any less of it, but the various categories are grouped together in smaller carrying bags and cases. I'm particularly fond of tool boxes. Easier access, packing ability, and less weight are the obsessive/compulsive results. Why does it make me so happy to do this?

Still no exercise besides walking, no French lessons but one, and I need them. I'm trying and want to be fluent, but my ability to form sentences has flown right out of my head—along with vocabulary and basic structure. My mind has been fried for months with our transition, but I think I'm recovering.

We have had one real day of being out in the city, though we didn't leave our apartment till two o'clock. First we went by the computer shop to check on the printer. I had to be sure it wasn't salvageable before we bought another. It wasn't, so we threw it in the trash can.

Later we rode the Metro to the Rue du Bac, where we feel happy and at home. We stayed at the Hotel Saint-Germain in this neighborhood four years ago, when we were on the last leg of our six-week trip with the girls. We have so many happy memories from that stay. Mother came and joined us, and I have a wonderful picture of our three generations sitting on the sofa in the stylish lobby. There was a white French Bulldog that we loved to cluck at and rub. Jules was his name. Jim and I paid the hotel a visit, and Daniel was manning the desk as before—but now Jules had a new pal, a black and white companion.

We walked down the handsome rue, enjoying the avenue, and turned right. I had a mission at the Musee Maillol, which is one of my Paris favorites. I'd seen the Frida Kahlo/Diego Riviera show there years before and bought one of the posters. It was now framed but back at home, and I wanted Frida to travel with me around France. So I bought myself another poster. While we were there, we toured the rather kinky exhibition of Christian Schad, and I do mean exhibition.

Jim had been dying to see the Matisse/Picasso show at the Grand Palais, but we couldn't try until today, plus we didn't have tickets. We rode the Metro to the magnificent Place de la Concorde just at twilight. The sky was washed in blue and pink, the Eiffel Tower sparkling. We crossed the many streets to the Champs Elysees, and precisely at 5 o'clock the white lights threaded through the trees up and down the street all lit at once. It was a moment exquisitely delivered and unplanned for us—with the Arc de Triomphe framing the twinkling boulevard at its end. Yes, this was Paris!

The Palais was crowded, but we got in. Jim managed it free with his Writer's Guild card and telling the cashier that he was working, and he was. I always prefer Matisse to Picasso, although there were some Picassos I greatly enjoyed, and of course, many Matisses. But what made the show was its set-up—a conversation between the two artists. That's the notion that was so interesting, although it's hard to see any art with people herding through. A crowd like that makes me want to flee, and we did.

That night I actually took time to read for pleasure—*My Blue Notebooks* by Liane de Pougy, one of the famous Paris courtesans from the late 19th and early 20th centuries. This was Paris, after all, and it had been a good day in the city.

Once we were in bed and lulling to sleep, Jim coughed his head off. He was suddenly hacking and sick.

(HAPTER FIVE

Auntie Mame

BEFORE JIM WENT for his first art lesson, he was nervous as a schoolboy. He didn't know about these lessons, if this was the right atelier where he should be taking class. I offered to walk him, but he was afraid he might cling to my skirt (or more likely pajama tails) like Bret used to do. The really nice part was that he came back so pleased with himself. He once had a dream that he was in prison, and the only time he could get out was when he was painting. He enjoyed class, and the class enjoyed him.

A few days later, our favorite driver, Jacques, picked up Blair, Bret, and our friend Holly at the airport. The girls arrived for their Christmas vacation tired but peckish. I laid out their first French feast—pâté, fromage, baguette, clouds of the most luscious chocolate meringues, and cookies. We drank a welcoming toast of Champagne, and they all went to sleep while Jim went to class and I went to work.

That night we had dinner out, and the next day the girls slept very late while Jim and I took care of business. After lunch, we showed off our neighborhood to Blair and Holly, but Bret went back to bed. She'd just finished her first semester at Hollins University, driven back to Arkansas, then jumped on a jet. She had a lot of resting up to do.

Late the next afternoon—when the girls finally got up!—we all strolled to the Pompidou museum, which I'd never actually been to. I'd always thought it ugly until we went inside—until we rode the escalator to the top with Paris unfolding in front of us just at twilight.

Paris was magnificent from every step along the way, shimmering with lights, spreading its feathers. Of course the art was as breathtaking—a wonderful exhibition of Max Beckmann and a stunning permanent collection. The Pompidou instantly became one of my favorite museums.

Before we left, we had to have a drink at the rooftop Georges Bar. We sat in a yellow pod sipping our drinks and watching the new video exhibition, which was very Yellow Submarine-ish. There can't be a more romantic restaurant in Paris for dinner. The staff is hip and accommodating, tables are sleek and moderne, glass surrounds you as do the twinkling lights of the city. Surely, the food is good...but who cares!

The girls are sleeping like slugs, and who can blame them with the change in their bodies' clocks and the constant gray of Paris? Here in December it hardly seems like day even when it is. The sun comes out only occasionally.

I promoted the idea of visiting Sacre Coeur. Despite some grumbling on the girls' part, we walked, then rode the Metro and walked some more, climbed stair after stair, and finally made it huffing and puffing. Dark had descended, and the white basilica was washed in lights. As a soaring aerie in the black Paris sky, Sacre Coeur looked like the palace of a great sultan—which, in a way, I guess it is. The interior was laden with rich blue and gold, and nuns dressed in white habits with black headdresses began singing, a chorus of angel voices wafting to the heavens above. We all sat and listened, mesmerized.

On the Metro platform on our way home, a drunk man paced back and forth, lifting his leg and stretching and preening, getting into our space. Blair was ready to bop him with her bag if he got too weird. Bret was stifling a laugh. Once we boarded the car, Blair and I were talking, and we somehow interrupted a beggar's diatribe. "Please, shut up!" he yelled, and we obeyed. I was tempted to give him money so he would shut up. Our Sacre Coeur pilgrimage had turned into Nut Day.

The next day marked our three-week anniversary of being in Paris and the first time we'd seen someone from home—Winston Vickers and his wife, Susan. Winston is an old family friend, one of my brother Blair's best friends growing up. He's lived in California for many years, and I hadn't seen him in a very long time.

When Jim and I met up with them, Winston was standing outside his hotel on the Ile St. Louis looking like Winston but with a beard. He didn't recognize me at first, with my neon orange hair. We found an intimate restaurant and caught up about ourselves and our families with a crisp bottle of white wine and good food. Winston and Susan are changing their lives too—closing businesses, getting more degrees, and deciding on new ways to approach the world. Brave new beginnings all round in this confluence of past and present, Arkansas, California, and France.

Afterward, Jim and I met the girls at Le Bon Marche, with all the glorious foods at La Grande Epicerie de Paris turning our heads this way and that, so many choices with so little time, a gourmet menagerie that leads to indecision of what exactly to buy—although no indecision about sampling the Veuve Cliquot.

We rode the Metro home—nutless this time—ate a snack, ordered some pizzas, and stayed in. Bret was disappointed because she'd been dying to go to the Moulin Rouge this trip, and there was no room in our schedule. Plus she has parents who are writers and artists and chasing Matisse around France. The Moulin Rouge is $130 a pop. I promised her we'd go the next time.

I've always wished to give my children a big view of the world, and I've tried to do that their whole lives. I don't like to be told no. I don't like boundaries. I don't like being put in a pigeon hole. I want to be Auntie Mame and to crack the world open for myself and for those I love.

CHAPTER SIX
Ghosts of Christmas Past

THERE WAS CHASING and hiding. Children and their mothers were being put in...something...and being told they were being sent...somewhere. I felt the fear of the mothers and their children, fear of my own.

Whoever it was shut the door and threw, pushed, dumped what turned out to be a submarine into the water with the women and children—and me—in it. It sank. It was meant to be a coffin. Someone (maybe me) cracked one of the windows with a high-heeled shoe. Water came rushing in, and we all knew we would die. The mothers wanted to protect their children, and they couldn't.

The dream stopped, and my eyes were open like I was looking out into the bedroom. There was a wispy ghost—not fashioned as a person, but whimsically created as a Japanese kite—sailing through the room. Then there were others floating by me. Many, many, many came and went, but I was not afraid. Suddenly, somehow I had the feeling these ghosts were Jewish children from the Marais whom the Nazis took and killed, and they wanted my attention. They wanted me to write about them. This dream that came from thin air, or somewhere in my head, was about the Nazis murdering these children.

Could this be true? I have no idea. I only know the simplest history about this area, but there is a Jewish Museum a few blocks away. I must try to go. But if my dream is true, and the wispy kites of children called me, I have done as they wished.

* * *

WE WOULD HAVE to leave Perche on December 27th, the day Blair and Bret were flying back to Arkansas. Where would we go? I'd been dealing with that major issue only a little, emailing back and forth with Randall Vemer of French Home Rentals, who had become our immediate and stalwart supporter when he first read about our project. He'd been contacting more of his company's property owners to tell them about us and *Chasing Matisse*, trying to help find us another place to stay. One interested couple was going to lend their beautiful apartment, and then it rented. I believed something would work out— that something would fall out of the sky to save us, just as Perche had.

Another reason I hadn't dealt with this primary issue more is that it requires a certain kind of energy for me to put my neck on the chopping block. I don't always have it. I must feel rested, energetic, positive, able to withstand rejection. I have to have some reserves in order to put myself out there. As I writer, I've put my neck on that line what seems like zillions of time, and it's gotten chopped off plenty. It's never easy. You never get used to it: Even when you think it won't matter, it does. I hadn't had that kind of energy until the day Holly left, and we all rested and reorganized ourselves.

Money, or more accurately the lack of it, has been a draining stress and burden in our lives, especially for the last few years. It has paralyzed us, depressed us, instilling fear and doubt about ourselves, creating any number of problems for us and between us, complicating our lives in untold ways. Fear is the worst—destructive and debilitating. Jim and I have written and believed, hoped, wished, and persevered on the paths of what we're called to do. That's what artists do.

We've believed in ourselves and our work. We've bet on ourselves. We've made an investment in ourselves and our future, taken this risk of moving to France that many people would be afraid of. But in the process, we've created a lot of debt. *Chasing Matisse* is a hugely expensive project, and the book contract advance is long gone. Again, we're betting on ourselves.

Our first Christmas away from home, in Paris no less, wasn't feeling too Christmasy on the Eve itself. Our tradition is to have a delicious, spirited, and sparkling dinner with Champagne, oysters, standing rib roast, Yorkshire pudding, asparagus, garlic mashed potatoes, and a luscious dessert. Friends usually come for drinks, others stay for dinner. By the time it's over and we've cleaned up, it's 2 A.M. The next morning we're tired and excited, happy to be opening our presents—which are many though not grand. Our good dog, Snapp, is the most thrilled of all. He loves his gifts and expects them with tremendous anticipation. He can't wait to open the various treats, which are almost always food. I maintained the surprises of Santa Claus up until a year or two ago, and still and always will fill our stockings.

On this Christmas Eve, I planned for us to go to one of the beautiful florists and make an arrangement for our Christmas tree. We could each choose our botanical desires. The place I had in mind had big branches of holly which I wanted as my part of our tree collage. Blair chose an orchid and Bret a little pot of roses. The name of the shop was Art et Nature. We walked in, and the woman in charge didn't speak any English and didn't do anything but pout and roll her eyes and sigh loudly and with exasperation when we tried to speak French and explain the flowers we wanted. She had no Christmas spirit. We should've left, but I wanted one of those holly branches—but only one, since they were eight euros apiece.

Blair, Bret, and I went to pick up our Buche de Noel and a few more items. They had a fight (not unusual—I think we fight every year on Christmas Eve, until our party). When we got home, Jim was freaked out, almost catatonic. I didn't know what sent him reeling until a week later. I thought it was the income tax (he was also working on that) that had done him in. But he had received news that we had less money than he thought, and more bills had to be paid.

That evening we dressed up and rode the Metro to the Boulevard St. Germain where we had a dinner reservation at Vagenende—which had been highly recommended. Coming out from the Metro we went the wrong way and arrived 40 minutes late, though the restaurant thought it more, since whoever answered the phone had failed to write down the change in the time of our reservation which I'd called in. They weren't happy with us either. The food was wonderful—briny oysters that tasted of the sea, and perfectly cooked fishes. A tart tapenade with crusts of bread was set on the table to start. We woofed it down.

We had planned to attend a midnight mass at Notre Dame, but the police had captured what they'd initially thought was a bomber with bombs there that afternoon, and we opted out. Instead, we went home and had our Buche de Noel and a glass of Champagne after midnight, but we were already too full.

Jim and I had told Blair and Bret that there were no presents this year. Their gift from us was the trip to Paris, and our gift from them was their coming. On Christmas morning we could all sleep late and not be rushed. So that's what we did. There were no presents, no anticipation, no event. It seemed sad and pathetic, which is what I told my mother when I called later in the day. I think that pleased her—in the sense that yes, we did indeed miss being with our family.

Jim and I went out into the world to pick up our order from La Fougasse and the Rotisserie Man. I loved that they were open Christmas Day. The French want their food nice and freshly cooked. Nothing much else happened except getting dressed and preparing the table for dinner. We had invited Ruben and Chloe to join us. Jim drew and painted decorations for our little tree, which made us all happy.

When our guests arrived, we popped Champagne. Over the next four or five hours, we laughed and talked and ate and decorated our makeshift tree, which became quite festive, as did we. It became Christmas after all, and the lesson to us is that yes, we want to have presents no matter what they are, and yes, we have to have a Christmas party. It's not Christmas until we do.

CHAPTER SEVEN

A Light in the Window

THERE WAS AN underlying sadness during Christmas week because my chicks were flying home. When Jim and I left Little Rock for France in late November, we at least knew we'd see one another again in only two and a half weeks. Now we were parting with no meeting planned.

I have chosen to be a nomad, but Bret has been forced; at least Blair has an apartment that doesn't shut for holidays. What Jim and I were doing was momentous—closing down 501 Holly in Little Rock, my daughters' childhood home, the place where our lives came together as a family, the house where they could walk in the door and their mama would cook them a meal and their stepfather would act silly with them. They could sleep in their own beds. The dog and cat would greet them with affection. Their clothes hung in their closets.

They felt safe.

Anyway, December 26th was a sad day, a working day, a packing day. The girls were leaving, and we had to move. Michel Tessel had been kind enough to offer Jim and me another apartment of his, Sante Croix, for a reduced rate. We hadn't found another place and decided a tiny hotel room wouldn't do.

We were to meet Ruben at 6 PM to retrieve a key and take some bags so the move wouldn't be so hard the next morning. It was only a few blocks away, so Jim, Blair, Bret, and I walked down the rue Vielle du Temple pulling a suitcase each, and I'm not talking about little ones. I was laughing, thinking of the sight we must look. "The Joads of Paris!" I called to Jim.

"Jwahds," he called back, pronouncing it the French way.

After that, we trekked to Montparnasse and La Closerie des Lilas, a classic restaurant that's been restored to its former glory. We had drinks at the bar, me sitting on Hemingway's stool while the expert bartender, in white jacket and black tie, shook his cocktails. We decided to dine there for our last supper together.

Bret woke up vomiting the next morning. I called and wrangled with Delta Airlines and finally got her on a flight a day later. It turned out to be a freight run. Guess that agent didn't like it when I asked to speak to her supervisor, but what's one to do when there's no intelligent bending of rules?

Jacques picked up Blair, and we said teary goodbyes as she left without her sister. Then Jim, Bret, and I moved, bag by bag, from Perche to Sante Croix—Bret's pot of flowers, our Christmas tree, the food in the refrigerator. It was exhausting, up and down flights of stairs. But we got it done.

Bret slept. I reorganized and wrote. Jim ventured into the rain to try and take care of business and came home wet and beaten. Then I went out to hunt and gather chicken soup and crackers for my girl. We watched bad French TV, which often consists of bad American reruns.

The next morning Jacques came to get Bret. By noon, I felt her illness and crawled into her bed, took medication, and slept for hours.

* * *

OVER THE NEXT few days, Jim and I began preparing to leave Paris on our grand adventure of driving around France pursuing Matisse. We arranged with Jacques to accompany Jim in picking up the car in early January. And we convinced Monsieur Michel Malric at our favorite boutique hotel, the Hotel Saint Germain, to let us leave suitcases in his cave and receive mail at the hotel. "You have a home in Paris," he said. "On the rue du Bac. Not bad."

It was good to take our minds off our troubles and our absent loved ones. We'd been so busy we'd hardly had any time to enjoy Paris. And now we were about to leave it! Even in the winter gray, Paris is a vision that both dazzles and charms. I see her as an elegant lady with grand and timeless style.

One day Jim and I crossed the Seine to the Left Bank and wound through the streets according to our fancy. People were out in droves. We looked up Shakespeare & Co., which is not Sylvia Beach's store but retains the Lost Generation aura and draws the literary crowd. It was teeming with Lost Generation wannabes—including us. The rue de la Huchette was wall-to-wall Greek tavernas and kiosks, with the enticing aromas of grilling pigs and lambs on turning spits. We were hungry, and like everyone else in this city, we stopped to pick up a snack to munch as we walked.

We had a drink at Les Deux Magots, which is always in fashion, even if you're sitting with the other tourists trying to pretend you're not one of them. After that we ambled around the Left Bank, where we used to stay but had missed this time. During our weeks in Paris we'd walked the streets at night looking in art gallery windows, encountering lots of mediocre art—but also, in hotel and restaurant windows, an exhibition poster featuring a wonderful painting called "Anemones et grenades" by an artist named Pierre-Humbert. Jim had been captivated by the colors and style of this picture, which we'd only seen on the posters.

Then, on that cold, rainy, late-December Sunday night, we suddenly turned a corner and I saw it. It was on an easel in the window of Galerie Daniel Besseiche at 33, rue Guenegaud. Jim was beside himself. And I took a picture of him with the painting that he calls "the best art I've seen in Paris galleries." We didn't yet know how much of an impact this discovery would have on our "chasing Matisse." For now, it was just a bit of much-needed warmth and color after all our travails. As Jim said, "It's like a light in the window."

CHAPTER EIGHT

Here Comes The Sun

THE DIVA STEPPED into the light, her bearing regal, her posture erect. It was 2 o'clock on New Year's Day, and we'd chosen to set a cultural tone for our 2003 start on this adventure to find the creative life, to see ourselves and the world in new ways, to shake and rattle the lethargy in our systems. We sat in folding chairs of the Eglise Saint-Julien-Le-Pauvre, the oldest sanctuary in Paris and one of two Greek Melkite Catholic parishes. The lighting was subdued as Catherine Manandaza thrilled us through Mozart and Ave Maria, and the chamber orchestra of violin virtuosos flawlessly performed Vivaldi's Four Seasons.

The next day Jim began this new season of our lives by heading back to Galerie Daniel Besseiche and Pierre-Humbert's painting. He'd hoped to meet and talk with Monsieur Pierre-Humbert, but the gallery representative, Alice Pennington-Mellor, told him the artist had died 10 years before. With good luck in timing, though, Jim met Pierre-Humbert's widow—who just happened to have a rendezvous that day at the gallery!

Later that week the two of us went back for a follow-up conversation. Anne Pierre-Humbert is a beautiful woman with blue eyes that are as light filled as her late husband's paintings. Her face is framed by a well-cut gray pageboy, and her spirit carried us away with its effervescence. As Alice kindly translated, Anne spoke of Pierre-Humbert and their life together. She was an actress who performed on the radio when they met. Pierre knew her voice before he ever laid eyes on her. They lived most of the year in Paris, though they had a summer and holiday house in the South. It is such a civilized life.

Many of their friends were artists as well, and even when they were competitive, they supported one another. After an opening, they would all go out to dinner together. Pierre-Humbert said this was the last of the good artist times. Anne believes artists were more supportive of one another then than now. Money was sometimes hard to come by, but when they needed it the most, a miracle would happen. "When you are doing the work you love," she said, "you may not live as well, but it's all you need."

Anne said Pierre-Humbert always looked for the light in his paintings, and I could see what she meant. His paintings resonated with color, life, and light. I admire his images, which seemed to me "suggestions" of the scenes and objects he painted and dreamed.

Alice has become our dream-maker as well. It had been eight long weeks since I'd gotten a haircut or color. I looked like a shaggy ghost of myself and was so mentally exhausted I couldn't figure out what to do. Alice came to my rescue and organized a hair appointment down her street. But the best of all is that she believes she may be able to help us find a house in Brittany, where Jim can paint and write for a while when we're on the road. Genie, genie, come again, let dear Alice bring us a house!

Back at the apartment, we had an email from our sweet friend Patti. She'd rented out our house in Arkansas for a month! Our accountant had also sent a message: "Don't worry, be happy," it said.

This was such a great day. We received gifts of hope, courage, and kindness from people we knew and others we'd never laid eyes on. One expects friends and family to be supportive, but the generosity of strangers is stunning. These people I've described don't know us, but they understand our dream and adventure, and are helping us make it come true.

* * *

ON A DAY when Paris was glistening with pink light that somehow floats in the sky—the first day in six weeks that's truly been clear and sunny—we were waiting for Alice at the Place d'Italie. Jim had walked across the street to an ATM, and I was eyeing a Kentucky Fried Chicken restaurant in front of me. We hadn't eaten American food since we'd been in France, and I'd been craving KFC ever since we saw one in Les Halles. Alice was taking us to Anne Pierre-Humbert's apartment to see Pierre's studio and we wanted to bring Anne a gift. I was thinking a bucket of chicken would be nice...and, by the way, I'd like to have some. Instead, we stopped into a chocolaterie and bought a golden box of bonbons and a bag of pate de fuits.

Anne's small apartment was simply and tastefully decorated, with one wall of windows. Art was everywhere we looked—Pierre-Humbert's paintings, sculptures, drawings, and the fine and beautiful cups Anne served our coffee in. It turns out she's an artist, too, and the cups are her graceful work.

Pierre-Humbert once had an exhibition in South Carolina, she said, and they made the trip there.

Even though he probably spoke better English than she did, she was the one who talked for both of them. We discussed the fact that women are the ones who stick their necks out. We're the braver of the sexes. While Pierre-Humbert and Anne were in the U.S., they also visited New York. When they returned to Paris, it seemed like a village to her. I thought that a perfect description.

After our coffee and cookies, she led us up a flight of stairs to Pierre-Humbert's studio. Stacks of paintings, folders of drawings, and photographs of his work held the room in his energy. The chaise where Pierre-Humbert set his nudes was left undisturbed, and a bookshelf was filled with volumes devoted to Matisse (also Pierre-Humbert's great inspiration). In fact, he and Anne made a pilgrimage to the Matisse Museum in Nice once a year. Pierre-Humbert's atelier was a living vision of his work—and of his and Anne's life together. The afternoon was an honor and a treat for us.

Afterwards, we rode the bus to the Galerie Besseiche, we three women sitting in a back corner giggling like girlhood friends. I felt lucky to be with them. Jim wasn't included in this female club and sat across from us. But I could tell he was happy, the sun through the bus window warming his face. No wonder whole cultures have worshipped the giver of radiance, when illumination returns after the darkness of night, and the world is given back to them. That's how it is for Jim on this day when the orb finally makes an appearance. The sun drenches him with its rays, and his dark night lifts as well, his moroseness gone.

In many ways the sky feels brighter today, an absolutely perfect day. Two more to go before we leave Paris!

CHAPTER NINE

Northern Exposure

I 'M HAPPY NO one knows where we are. It's not like people can't call or email, but now that we're out of Paris and in the countryside, it feels like we're not so in touch. All the hard news comes from the States, and we need a rest after the intensity of the last six weeks. Chasing Matisse is our passion, but starting a new life here is made harder by the fact that our house hasn't sold—that beautiful house that delighted everyone who walked through its door. Everyone on this side of the Atlantic who sees pictures is wowed by it. I have to believe that its failure to sell is due to some cosmic reason that we don't yet understand. Whoever has the excellent fortune to buy 501 Holly will find it filled with good energy—a happy and remarkable home.

When we arrived at the village of St. Quentin, in Picardie, we didn't have a hotel reservation. We didn't even know if we would stay in St. Quentin or drive on to one of the smaller towns where Matisse was born and grew up. But after touring the centre ville, we decided to use St. Quentin as our base. Plus, the Hotel des Cannoniers called to us as we drove by it. As we now know, Monsieur and Madame Michels bought their classical manor in sad disrepair and spent four years renovating it—making it into a stunning home as well as a lovely hotel. Our first room was really a suite with a well-turned-out kitchenette on the top floor.

Very writerly, we thought, and a fine place to work. We later had to change rooms to accommodate a longstanding reservation. Our second room was elegant with a perfect view of the garden. Oh, joy! Oh, perfection! We have exited the city without reservations and landed here! The nomads did well. And, even better, we did well for a good price. Next morning Jim couldn't find the car keys. After breakfast, we visited the local police station to see if anyone had turned them in. The friendly gendarme pulled out a huge box of lost keys, but none were ours. We'd planned to drive to Matisse's birthplace that morning, but instead found ourselves with a forced day off. Back at the hotel, we took our third French lesson on CD since arriving in France. We got CNN at the hotel, the first time we'd seen it since being in France. It was good to hear the news in English—for a short time. But I didn't really want to know what was going on in the world. I wanted to deal with my life day to day. I wanted to chase Matisse without politics.

We prepared a lunch of good cheeses and hummus and crispy whole wheat rolls. Afterwards, I was lying on the bed reading when Jim suddenly said, "Here's the extra key!" It was stuck in an obscure slot of his briefcase. We stepped out to the automobile we'd had for two days to search for the vital master key with clicker to lock and unlock the doors. They weren't there, but we almost didn't care. At least we could drive the car.

Now Jim dug though his briefcase once more. This time he sheepishly held up the missing keys. There's no question: The lost keys just didn't want to be found. We have so many bags and sacks, Jim has so many pockets, it was easy for them to hide. Plus with our minds spinning in so many directions, it's hard to keep up with where we put what. But at this point we were sticking to our plan—to lie down for a nap. It's a treat to be in such a pleasant place and allow ourselves this rare luxury—a day of rest.

The next day was big—we were headed for Le Cateau-Cambresis, the small village where the Musee Matisse had recently opened after being closed for many years. Matisse was born in this village, then his family moved to Bohain a few kilometers away. The Picardie sky was gray as we drove through miles of beet fields. Hard to believe the painter known for his color came from land like this.

What a surprise the museum was! Quite grand for this tiny place, with a huge and lovely garden in back. We were lucky to arrive during a special exhibition of the famous French editor Teriade, who enticed his talented and famous friends—Bonnard, Chagall, Giacometti, Gris, Le Corbusier, Leger, Matisse, Miro, Picasso, Rouault, and many others— to paint, draw, and write for his publication, Verve. In the permanent Matisse exhibit, we came across classes of schoolchildren huddled on the floor with paper and pencils. They studied Matisse's brilliant work and drew their own versions. What a privilege for these children, what vision on the part of the museum and teachers. How might this visit change their ability to see the world?

The first time I accepted calling myself an artist was on our six-week trip to France in 1998. I felt an admiration for artists here, and I identified with the thread that binds creative people together: the language that we use to speak about our work—the conception, construction, and the end result. Now, at this Matisse museum, I was filled with the sensation of these men (and they all were, I think), these artists, creating their impression of their worlds. They put down on paper whatever childish, mysterious, beautiful, humorous, or dark images they saw in their inner and outer eyes, the ones that spoke to them—and now to us. They were compelled and not afraid for their visions to be exposed, their voices to be heard. This inspired me and reaffirmed my feeling about my own work. It makes me want to free myself, to express myself with abandon. Not to worry about the demands of fitting into a pigeon-hole, a mold of expectation (which I don't until rejection makes me doubt myself). It's the daring to be true to yourself—to be authentic—that is essential, no matter what form your art takes.

This is what all real artists face.

CHAPTER TEN
Each Step I Take

IT'S HILARIOUS SEEING "The Simpsons" in France—Homer and Marge speaking French with Bart and Lisa, and better than Jim and I do. As irony would have it, we saw an episode in a hotel room in Rouen, in which the Simpsons somehow go back in time to 15th-century France (since they were speaking *Francais*, I didn't quite get how). But Lisa becomes Joan of Arc. And there we were in the city where Joan was burned at the stake.

The next morning we were off to Étretat, on the Normandy coast. We tried to listen to our French CD in the car, but it almost put us to sleep after our fine lunch. The most interesting village we passed through on the way was Fécamp, which has been a fishing port for centuries. It's built on a hillside leading down to the harbor on the English Channel. Fishermen sailed first on schooners, and now trawlers, from here to Newfoundland to catch the cod in cold, fog, and bad seas. As is the case in such towns, where men have made their livings from the deep, many never returned—lost in icy waters. It's one of those ways of life that is fascinating to me—the mysteries of oceans and the people who live by and from them.

In Étretat we drove straight to the Dormy House hotel. It seemed deserted but was open, and we checked in. The sea was forever in front of us, the famous cliffs (which I knew nothing about before Matisse) on either side with the village nestled between. Our room was large and cheerful with two sets of French doors opening onto a balcony—and a perfect view of the sea, the cliff, and the little church perched on top of it. This was a room in which Jim could hardly wait to paint.

After getting settled, we walked down through the village and up the steps and path to the church. What a haul. But when we reached the thick, green crest, we were on the top of the world. The cliffs go on as far as the eye can see, sheer walls of rock with sharp drop-offs to the ocean below. There are steps down through the crags and then back up, which we climbed with heaving breaths. The sky turned pink for a glorious sunset on the horizon. We've noticed pink in the light and sky here almost every day. You see this in paintings many times, and it is not exaggerated. With this space and beauty and light, it becomes obvious why so many artists and writers came here to work.

The next day Jim sketched on the cliff, and I wrote in our room with the spectacular view. We lunched on Port Salut and Roquefort cheeses, sausage, ham, and toasts. That afternoon Jim set up his easel by the window and got out his oils. A huge yellow cat stepped lightly in from the balcony to watch him. It has been fine for us to be working in such close quarters, which is a miracle. I'm like a radio antenna that picks up sensory information from everyone around me—especially those I love. Sometimes this energy is so intense that I can't feel myself, or identify whose craziness it is—mine or whoever else's. Jim is moody, which can throw me for a loop. I've learned how to handle this better in the last few years. And with help from my Wise Women friends, I'm understanding how to take care of myself.

It's dark at 8 A.M. here. Not pitch black, but the lights of the village are still on, which makes it hard to get up from this luxurious bed. Man, have we slept in some nice ones—mattresses with just the right firmness and padding, crisp linens that make crawling under them an instant of bliss—usually between midnight and 1 A.M. for me. We leave the French door cracked to hear the surf lapping the beach. I usually work late after dinner, writing and trying to catch up with email, which is our source of communication—that and the phone. Even though I bought stamps in Paris, we haven't sent one post card or letter.

I force myself out of bed and run a hot bath, wishing it were infused with bubbles, but I have none. Instead, I submerge my body in clear water. Jim sketched on the cliff, and then we went to the village for a lunch of ham and cheese galettes and cidre—which is alcoholic cider, I think lighter than beer, more refreshing to me with its effervescence. Cidre is served in a tea cup, this one without handle.

After lunch we drove into the hills to look at the mansions. Étretat is a pretty village, no doubt more so in Spring. Most of it is shut up for the season, but that's okay—Jim and I like to be in places in winter when no one else is there, when the leaves have fallen from the trees and the sky is clear and cold. Here the sun and clouds and rain take turns. Within minutes the weather changes, blowing in and out across the Channel.

In the last couple of days, Jim and I were having a conversation and I said, "Each step I take is a step I've never taken before." He loved that. It popped out of my mouth before I really thought about it. But now that I have, I find it an accurate description. What I'm realizing is that this act, spirit, consciousness, vision—whatever it is—is critical for my sense of well-being. I'm not sure I knew this about myself when I was younger, or maybe I've grown this way with age. I did understand from the first time I landed in Europe that I wanted to live on this continent someday. I feel more fulfilled and engaged here than I did at home.

CHAPTER ELEVEN
When It Feels So Right

I'VE HAD A couple of breakdowns about the choices we've made, where we'll end up. Second guessing and questioning how we'd gotten ourselves to the point where we are (and I don't mean in France—I mean how stretched we are financially). Isn't there some song lyric that says, "When it feels so right, how can it be wrong?" That sums it up.

I arrived in picturesque Honfleur feeling like a wreck. We'd been here years before with Blair and Bret, savoring a lunch of fish under an awning by the harbor while it drizzled rain. The waiter had flirted with Blair. Today the sun was out, and the streets were semi-crowded with people. We looked for a hotel. We finally stopped at the L'Ecrin, which we'd been by several times. It called to me. When we walked in, a jovial French woman, Daniele, greeted us warmly. We explained what we're doing—chasing Matisse—and she excitedly told us she had a friend who'd been one of Matisse's models. She lived not far away. What luck! This was striking gold! Daniele immediately picked up the telephone and called Madame Mickels, handed the phone to Jim, and they made an appointment to meet the next day. The L'Ecrin is lovely, the kind of place I'm drawn to anyway, but of course, I now believe our finding it was meant to be.

We were shown to an exquisite room with wallpaper of blue and yellow flowers, gold drapes and bedspread. Silk and lace curtains were pulled to the bedposts—no canopy, and the marbles in the bathroom matched the blue and gold details—our loveliest room yet. Jim went to sketch, and I went to sleep.

I believe it's true that you create your own reality. Oh, Fairy Godmother, this golden bedroom is how I picture mine.

After a dreamy night on that luscious bed, we had breakfast delivered to our room. It came with an orchid—purple splashed on white: perfect. Jim sketched his heart out in that room, he loved it so. Now this is the Matisse I wanted to find. Jim is happy, happy, happy when his art is flowing. Two aspects of Matisse's work that we both love are all the patterns and colors in the captured space. This room had that kind of detail and beauty, and Jim was inspired by it. He, like his hero, likes to paint interiors.

I worked. I bathed. I dressed—all so Frida and I could frolic in the garden before the appointment with Madame Mickels. It was gray and misting, but we didn't care. It was a garden of delight with tiny hidden vistas of cherubs and handsome carved bench and what I am going to call a French pagoda. We could see an easel through the glass, and Frida and Jim argued over who would get it if the studio belonged to us. What a place to paint! I had to intervene.

Jim had a conversation with Daniele and reported back to me that Madame would be here at noon to meet us. Having heard part of their interchange (and with my superior knowledge of the French language), I was suspicious of this message. It really didn't make sense, but we waited for a while. Jim amused himself by sketching, as I was snooping around. As time went on, I decided to speak up. I suggested he may not have understood what she'd said, and that we better sort it out so we could have a little lunch. He went off to find Daniele.

Aha, what I thought had happened, had: Daniele had asked Jim if he had an appointment with Madame, and he said, yes. She then inquired of its time. Monsieur Bubba thought Danielle was requesting the time of day, and he responded, 12:00 P.M. We waited for the Madame who would not come until this mix-up got unmixed. Then Daniele called Madame Mickels, and we set an appointment at her house later on.

We didn't try any of the fancier restaurants in Honfleur. Frankly, we were ready for simpler food in relaxed surroundings—no fussiness. We drove down to the harbor and chose, of the few restaurants open,

L'Ancrage. A green salad with tomatoes and our first soupe de poisson (fish soup). I love soups and stews, big pots of things. We got a steaming bowl with croutons, grated cheese, and rouille in bowls. This is a ritual I now love. First, the croutons sprinkled on top, cheese on them, and rouille in dollops. Yum.

We used Danielle's directions to find the appointed meeting place, and Madame Mickels stepped out of her little car with flaming red hair, a band wrapped around it, wearing jodhpurs, a sweater adorned with pearls, and tall boots. Her big dog waited in the back seat. Madame is quite beautiful, a tiny woman who carries herself gracefully. We followed her down a narrow road to her house in the country.

Janie Mickels met Matisse in 1940. She'd heard him speak on the radio, cheering the young people of France to keep working and to have courage. (This, of course, was during the war.) Jim will tell the story of how they actually met and give the scoop on what Madame revealed to us about her revered friend and mentor, but the bottom line is that she became Matisse's model (of many paintings we have seen) and his art student. She had stacks of books, letters, articles, and pictures—a treasure trove of materials. They remained friends until his death in 1954.

We pored over books with drawings and paintings Matisse made of this charming Madame. She is an accomplished artist herself with exhibitions in Paris and in Honfleur. (She was also a great friend of Maurice Chevalier and showed us a wonderful picture of them together.) I took photos. We talked and talked. It was a successful afternoon, and we kissed goodbye. Jim and I were elated!

All it takes is for a little something to go right—a chance meeting, a charming street, a sunshiny day, a moment of beauty, in whatever form—and I feel like we're back on track again.

CHAPTER TWELVE
The Spirits of Belle Ile

THIS WAS THE day Jim had been waiting for. We were going to Belle-Ile-en-Mer, an island in the Atlantic off the Brittany Coast which was important for Matisse's artistic development. Jim had been dying to get here, and to make it even better, we would land on Belle Ile on his birthday. He always hates his birthday—but not this one.

Everyone who knows the island has told us how beautiful it is, another French venue I'd never heard of until we were introduced by Monsieur Matisse. The day couldn't have been more perfect. The sky was clear and blue, and we drove onto the ferry at the seaside town of Quiberon. I don't care how cold it is, I have to be on the top deck to look out at the sea and feel the ocean breeze. I love boats and ships and being on the water. I think it's a great way to see any place where a body of water is the eau de vie. We bundled up. Some people moved down a deck, but not us.

As the ferry pulled into Le Palais, the capital of Belle Ile, the Citadelle Vauban loomed in front of us. Its massive walls have guarded Belle Ile for centuries.

There were boats in the harbor, and like in other French ports the quay was lined with hotels and eateries. We couldn't check into our inn, so we found a restaurant with a fantastic view of the harbor and ordered a dozen oysters each with a bottle of crisp Muscadet. Our next course was more soupe de poissons. Crème caramel for dessert. What a birthday lunch! I couldn't think of anywhere in the world I'd rather be. More importantly, neither could the birthday boy.

We realized we were right by Matisse's address in Le Palais and looked it up. The building was in front of us—a patisserie on the ground floor where Matisse resided in the attic. He and Madame Matisse lived in lots of attics until the money started rolling in.

Since we were so close, we decided to check out the citadel. Monks first built a monastery on this rocky point in the 11th century. Later, fortifying efforts were begun—but after Belle Ile had been attacked so many times by the British and Dutch, Louis XIV sent the engineer Vauban there in the 17th century to plan the island's defense.

This fort is huge and high and thick. We read that Alexander Dumas had spent time in Belle Ile, and when you see this citadel, you know where the Count of Monte Cristo came from. It is so Monte Cristo. The German Army occupied it during World War II, and it was rather creepy to walk through—which adds to the intrigue. From here, the view of the sea and Le Palais are stunning, and the museum is full of interesting tidbits. My favorite item was—if my limited reading of French is accurate—the lid of one of local resident Sarah Bernhardt's hatboxes. The green areas are pristine with palm trees and succulent plants as big as dining room tables.

Well, we had to have a nap after that. Those bottles of wine at lunch wear you out, so we checked into our peaceful inn, Le Clos Fleurie.

For dinner, Alice had recommended a restaurant in Sauzon called La Maison. She wouldn't give us details but said we would love it. Sauzon is only a few kilometers from Le Palais, and it didn't take long to get there. We walked into the bar and at the opposite end of the room was a cozy conversation area with a fireplace. People were drinking aperitifs in front of a wood fire. Oh-*kay*.

La Maison is immediately charming, but it takes a while to notice all the funny details. I'm not going to give the secrets away to spoil anyone's surprise, but let's just say there were mousetraps that Jim first thought were for catching vermin. His astonishment was a condiment to my dinner. We had our own aperitif—yet another Kir, this made with Cassis and a sparkling Muscadet—while looking over the eclectic and enticing menu. I ordered a Thai crab bisque, while Jim had Corsican charcuterie. We shared an order of stuffed crabs. All the seafood is caught in the waters off Belle Ile. The dinner was smashing. Afterwards, we had a drink in the bar as some of the locals sang French songs. This was a festive birthday for Jim.

The next morning, we got in our Peugeot and drove first to Sauzon, which, as Jim would say, is charming as all get out. The beautiful harbor, boats, cottages all looked ideal. I would like to stay here sometime at a small hotel where a fairy godmother surely must live.

From there we went to the famous La Pointe des Poulains, which surpassed the oohs and ahs we'd been told about it. Gigantic boulders of rock with the stormy waves crashing into them, a huge green bluff with a lighthouse the only vertical line on its top, the rock infused with quartz. They looked like enormous oyster shells. We were stunned by the majesty. There was a fort across an inlet from us, and I suggested to Jim that we buy it and move in. That's how I see La Pointe des Poulains.

We drove on to another natural phenomenon, L'Apothicairerie, where Matisse once stayed in a hotel that is no longer standing. The same stormy seas crashed and sprayed on walls of rocks this time, more like the bluffs of Étretat. There is a path that goes around the whole island. You can hike all or part of it, but you can see it clearly here. It reminds me of the Cinque Terre in Italy—but with fewer tourists.

From there, we followed the signs to Kervilahouen to locate the house where Matisse once rented a room. We had a picture, and I spotted it immediately—which was thrilling to discover this known/unknown quantity.

You wonder how there can be more exhilaration, but there is. This island is wild and wonderful and filled with spirits, I believe. And I think they're happy ones who caught their freedom in this setting of sea, sky, and earth. In turn, they delivered it to us with crashing waves and golden vistas, with pink light and pixie dances of sun and rain.

CHAPTER THIRTEEN

The Island Lure

SUNDAYS ARE FAMILY days in France, days to relax and enjoy. We haven't done too much of that, but it seemed right today—our last on the island. We would relish it. For lunch, we went back to La Maison, where a white Boxer pooch with a brown eye patch met us at the door. A gigantic Golden Lab and a little black dog were with their owners at a table near ours, while the Boxer stood at the door and longingly gazed in. This would be a three-dog lunch, which pleased us very much.

After lunch, we stoked the fire and finished our wine in front of it. Frida joined us. It reminded her of the cantinas she frequented in her old Mexico days. When we told Frida of the smartly placed fort at Pointe des Poulains—the one we wanted to own—she said, *You ninitos* (I think that's ninnies in Spanish), *that's the Fort de Sarah Bernhardt which she bought and made her summer home. Sarah loved Belle Ile.*

Of *course*, Jim and I chimed together. We had to go back—Frida was dying to pay the chanteuse a visit. Frida always knew they'd get along famously, and so they did. We wandered all around Sarah's beloved fort and imagined the parties with clever patter, ladies fitted in haute couture, singing and dancing, sparkling Champagne—all with crashing waves in the background.

I've been interested in Ms. Bernhardt since reading Liane de Pougy's *Blue Diaries*. The two women knew each other, ran in some of the same circles, and turned Paris on its ear in their own ways. Liane greatly admired Sarah's golden voice and skills on stage, and Sarah had given Liane acting lessons. After a few sessions, she told Liane that she had no talent and better stick to her beauty and dancer's turns on stage—and that that would be enough. Liane never said a bad word about Sarah that I recall, which is saying a lot, because Liane was scathingly honest in her diaries—about herself and everyone else. Frida pointed out that she was no wallflower either and fit right in. But Liane wasn't here today. It was Sarah, Frida, and me—three tempestuous women on this turbulent sea. Jim knowingly stayed out of our way.

It doesn't take long to get anywhere on Belle Ile. The island is small enough to be intimate and large enough that not everyone knows everyone else. There are many happy diversions to occupy your interests—villages to visit, lunches and dinners to be had, walks along the wild, thrashing seas and rocky cliffs. You can't get lost. Every turn you make has a sign to send you everywhere else.

After Sarah's fort, we drove over to Port Goulphar, where wild Australian painter John Peter Russell had a big house filled with his children, wife, and parties galore. Matisse painted with Russell. Today, there are two excellent hotels here (one with a spa) that command another dazzling view of island and sea. I want to stay there too. I want to come back to Belle Ile many times. We would love to be here for the Summer, Winter, Fall, or Spring.

Finally, we drove to Locmaria on the other end of the island. Pheasants were grazing in the field with the sheep and lambs. It's very Celtic here. We heard stories of sorcery having been practiced at some time in this island's history.

More intrigue and mystery, more spirits floating through time and space to give this island its fairytale feel.

If you're born on an island like Belle Ile, I imagine you either love it immensely and can't imagine living anywhere else—or you want to flee. But who are the people who *choose* to move to this island in the Atlantic? Are they wounded souls who want to hide away—to be alone and escape the harshness of humanity, to find some peace? Peace is a hard commodity to come by, no matter where you happen to be, and people create islands for themselves without the benefit of ocean expanse. Is it the call of freedom that people hear? Isolation undoubtedly has its appeal, but the beauty of the island can't be discounted—a bucolic life surrounded by sea. Belle Ile is a community that fills up in the summer with Parisians, British, and Dutch who've discovered its secret and are drawn here as well.

I think of St. Francisville, Louisiana, where our friends Ellen and Kenwood live—a small town that we also find irresistible. It's an eccentric community dotted with live oak trees and hanging Spanish moss, darling shops, and B & B's, all the Louisiana joie de vivre. The residents in St. Francisville have also been pulled together in some way. They prefer to live on their island, which happens to be on land.

These are questions I pondered later that afternoon as I watched a diet show on TV. That was nice after my big lunch. I probably gained three pounds. And there were all these self-righteous dieters: I hate them all.

I felt unsettled. Why? Is it about leaving tomorrow, getting back to the continent and the regular world and all that that implies? I have loved the spirits and spirit of Belle Ile, but I also miss my daughters. I feel so far away from my chickadees at home who have flown my coop that I flew as well. I wish we had a date to meet.

But we don't. And tomorrow it's time to move on again, to make the crossing back across the expanse of ocean—and within ourselves.

CHAPTER FOURTEEN

The Borrowed Home

W E MET ALICE at a boulangerie in her village of Auray, where she lives when she's not working at Gallerie Daniel Besseiche in Paris. We jumped out of the car and hugged like we hadn't seen one another in years, instead of weeks; then we got back in and followed her to the house that she had so generously arranged for us to use for a month. Here Jim would actually begin writing his book.

The road wound through a housing development, around a curve, and out into pastureland. Finally Alice slowed down and made a left turn through a big blue gate. It was a country house, maybe once a farmhouse, with a patio and outbuildings. When Alice opened the front door, we entered a house that was large and lovely, old but not ancient. The owners had redone it beautifully.

A modern and good-looking kitchen with tile floors was open to the dining area, which had a long table and lots of chairs—ideal for a dinner party. The owner's paintings—his own work—adorned the downstairs walls with grace and vitality, a range of solid technique and styles. I'm going to call the living room Primal Breton, with hints of Africa and 30's chic. In the four upstairs bedrooms (including two for kids), modern furniture was mixed with antiques. In other words, we liked this English couple just from their stuff. What a place and space to work!

We unpacked the car again. *Everything* came out this time. Then we drove to the huge Le Clerc supermarket (like an upper-scale Walmart

Supercenter, except with a bar) and loaded up on groceries for a month in the country. We were ready to eat in for a change. I figured out how to work the stove and slid turkey legs and thighs in the oven to roast, along with a mélange of vegetables. We opened a delicious bottle of Chinon and listened to music as we ate. Jim insists on candlelight at every evening meal.

Afterwards, he picked up a guitar he found and softly played and sang the songs he knows so well. As for the tempestuous two who were left, Frida found a perch in the living room that suited her, while I lay back on the sofa. We didn't have our own fort, but we had settled into another family's home.

Now that we were to be in one place for a month, I was happy to have a nest. I was even glad to cook again. This domestic act of preparing food touches me to earth. Since we'd been in France, this was the first time we'd had a kitchen in which whole meals could be made, with lots of pots and pans and room to chop and mix and a dishwasher to put the dirty dishes in. Roasting the turkey was the Thanksgiving we didn't have. There was just no time the day before we left the U.S. We had too much to try and finish up and still didn't get it all done.

Jim set his sights on an upstairs bedroom to open his laptop, hunker down, and start writing. I preferred the living room as my office. I could lay everything out on the long coffee table with the sofa as my chair. We both liked the kitchen but didn't feel it was the right spot. It became the neutral base. How appropriate. That's what kitchens always are—the heart of the home, where life is lived, meals are made, where people drop their defense shields, gather and converse, or fight with life-altering utensils within grasp.

The sky changes in a matter of minutes here—from blue skies to stormy clouds to drizzling rain, sometimes even hail and snow. It's fascinating to watch, a show that comes on every day, which is good since not only do we have bad French television, we also have bad Italian television. There's also some tragic Eastern European soap opera that is narrated. Strange. I require background noise while I write. Usually,

I prefer music—rock and roll, bluegrass, folk, Irish, Cuban, pop—whatever informs the mood of the work. Jim does that same thing, but he likes jazz and classical, which are usually too slow for me. I like my music loud, with a beat and wail.

But sometimes TV works fine. I don't really watch it, but still I'd like it to be a show I might watch—a movie, "Trading Spaces," "Oprah"—something like that. We had our own bad game shows (which weren't as silly as most of these) and talk shows at home, but I didn't watch them or turn them on for background noise. More channels, more choices—although there was something comforting about those old reruns of "Zorro" and "I Dream of Jeannie," even if they were in Italian.

At night, I sometimes watched French films (or American ones dubbed in French) and tried to improve my language skills. The kind owners of this house had two small children, so there were also kiddie movies available. I found myself turning on. *Cinderella*, starring Brandy, Whitney Houston, Jason Alexander, and Whoopi Goldberg; it was entertaining and well produced. (Really, who doesn't love a good Cinderella story?) And I was pleasantly amused by *The Borrowers*. I wished we had some of our own little Borrowers there. Brittany seemed perfect for them.

Being in these other peoples' home opened the issue of our own home, so far away. We had recently received word that our Realtor wanted to drop the price of our house. We hated the thought—we needed every cent we could get—but grudgingly said okay. The Universe is full of abundance and bounty, so how about sending some of it to us! We get FedEx in France, Universe. Do you have our new address?

CHAPTER FIFTEEN
A Part of Something

AFTER FOUR DAYS in the house, and I literally didn't walk outside for three, we decided it was time to start exploring this part of Brittany. One evening we drove into Auray to the port of St-Goustan. The St-Goustan Quartier is very old and charming, with the River Auray and 15th-century houses still standing, including one where Benjamin Franklin stayed when he came to France to negotiate a treaty with the French in 1776. Now Le Relais Franklin is a crêperie. Other restaurants and cafés line the quay. It was very dark and quiet on this night, but I was told that it could be quite lively in season.

The next Saturday we drove to Brittany's capital of Rennes and its weekly market. We'd been there once, years before, and wanted to visit again. Rennes is a city of 350,000 people and has an international air, with many cafés and brasseries. It was a beautiful day, and people were out in droves enjoying the sunshine. The market was huge and filled with so many choices that it took a few minutes to get the lay of it—to decide what you really wanted or needed.

It was just as we remembered—long lines of vendors with vegetables and fruits, one building with butchers and meat and another with cheese and birds, not to mention the huge fish bazaar and the mobile vendors of roasting birds and hot crêpes and galettes stuffed with cheese, ham, sausage, or something sweet coming off the smoking griddles. Jim and I were starving, and the first thing we did was line up to buy a galette. I feel grounded in an open-air market with the crops from the land, the farmers who grew them, and the other shoppers who appreciate this as well. People are friendly in markets. There's a sense of community. The earth is connecting us all. We filled bags and bags with leeks, celery, beets, carrots, green beans, pumpkin (or some gourd), mushrooms, apples, duck, thyme, cheese, and a huge chicken. The chicken I selected still had its head and feet. I sliced my hand across my neck and ankles to indicate to the jolly French woman that they had to go. I don't want to see a head attached to anything I eat. She also cleaned something out of it (I didn't want to know what) and prepared the gizzard and liver for us to take home. We've seen some spectacular sunsets here, but the one on our way back from Rennes was in a different league altogether. The sun looked like a giant burning pomegranate that was setting fire to the sea of clouds around it. Each second that it smoldered, the clouds went up in orange and pink smoke. The glow of the panorama changed constantly as this glorious brulée went on and on. There is nothing more inspiring than nature. It connects us primally to creation. Primitive cultures recognized and honored this, but with civilization we have mostly detached ourselves from this powerful force.

Speaking of primitive cultures, our borrowed house was just a few kilometers from the megaliths of Carnac, a display much larger than Stonehenge. One afternoon we went to see these thousands of stones standing in French fields. The signs guided us into the old seaside village of Carnac, which is charming and pristine. Deciding to get a little education before we viewed the stones, we went to the Musée de Préhistoire Miln-LeRouzic for some background. The museum's collection starts in the Lower Paleolithic and continues through the Early Middle Ages. There were a wealth of objects to check out (and handouts in English for the French-impaired).

The rocks themselves were mysterious. There were acres and acres of them, and the amount of work it took to create these alignments, dolmens, and tumuli of massive stones was striking. From serious to weird, myths abound of what the stones mean, how and why they were there—including that St. Cornely turned Roman soldiers into stone for persecuting Christians. (That doesn't sound very Christian to me, but everyone wants payback for something.)

Frida had to see as well, and so Jim and Frida and I walked through these fields and along these paths, wondering what our predecessors here had thought and felt. What does seem clear is that early man wanted meaning in life just as we do. It doesn't matter when or where you live, what your specific beliefs comprise, or how sophisticated you may be. There is a symbolic life and world and an effort to understand it. There is also a need to be part of something—a larger whole.

When I get in touch with who I am, and what we're trying to do, I feel grounded. I feel satisfied and happy. But it had been hard to find that place within or outside of myself in the past few weeks. This was a more internal time—which was both good and bad. In Paris, even if I worked all day, there was the pleasure at night of getting into the city's rhythm right outside our door.

But now the simpler quiet of the country was necessary. And it was fulfilling to move around with ease and to rest amid the trees and soothing green. But the humming, frenetic energy was missing. I knew that I needed it. I suppose there are some who like one rhythm or the other (and perhaps may fear to stray), but I require both.

That night Jim painted, then built a fire. He roasted fennel, baby turnips, and their greens with Poirée, olive oil, salt, pepper, and a fish we bought at a market. We talked about his paintings—authenticity, light, movement, color, space, design—and why we were there. This made me remember again and feel excited by it. I've always loved art and artists but have never thought a lot about it critically beyond the fact that I do.

Back when we were in Honfleur, Madame Mickels, Matisse's former model, said that Matisse's goal was to capture an emotion in his paintings. In thinking of these elements of art—emotion and the expression of it—I wondered again about Carnac and the mystery of the megaliths. Isn't this what the megaliths are as well, some way of connecting to the whole that we long to touch?

CHAPTER SIXTEEN

Letting Go

W E GOT AN offer on our house. It wasn't as much as we'd hoped for; not as much as we needed. But both our Realtor and our accountant advised us to accept it. So, with much anguish, we said yes. That night I cried in bed.

Now the movers were coming to our house in Little Rock to give us a bid. The whole idea threw me into a tailspin that left me scrubbing the oven in this borrowed house, while tears dripped from my nose into the toxic foam. Can you imagine how much I hate cleaning an oven? I was reduced to this horror, the most onerous domestic bore, to find some relief from worry over my furniture and other belongings.

Frida was purring: *But sweetie, we're in France! Nothing else matters.* Yes, Frida. It is wonderful! I love it here in our brave new world, my dream becoming fulfilled, and I couldn't ask for a better traveling companion than you. But what I find fault with is there—over the ocean: all those ties that aren't tied up, leaving us open to further emotional entanglement. Knowing something intellectually is the easy part— what's difficult is getting your head and heart in the same alignment. I believe that if we'd had the closure of the house selling before we left, it would've been hard—but easier than this. Over and done. Now, every action brings us closer to homelessness and the nomadic lifestyle our ancestors thousands of years before practiced—hunting and fishing, gathering berries, roots, and shellfish to live on. I prefer hunting and gathering at the BHV or Bon Marché, cute boulangeries or weekly markets.

Diego thinks you are silly, Frida said.

At least I can say this out loud: I know many people who cover their feelings (often with booze, pills, food, or meanness) so they can't feel them or be hurt again by someone else. I have done the same at times in my life, but I'd rather not now. But I frankly admit I feel sadness and grief—more lessons in letting go. This is what I wanted. I was ready to move onto and into a new chapter of my life. So what was I clinging to?

Several people told me they could never do what we were doing, because they would freak out without having a home. The idea of being homeless actually excited me, and still does—though making a wonderful home was very important to me, and probably will be again. If Jim and I are anywhere as long as a few days, we change furniture around to fit us. We make things comfy and homey. Am I freaking out?

Of course, Frida said. *If you didn't have children, would you feel the same?* She had a bit of attitude when she asked it.

I don't know. I definitely feel guilt because we don't have a "home" for them to come to. I wanted my children to be part of a strong family and to live in a solid home filled with beauty. Beauty is important in life—whether it's a moment or a sunrise, a fabric or a color, a piece of art or a piece of furniture, or a kind and generous heart. Beauty is essential to all of us, and my children had all that—though now they don't. Now they have to make their own homes in and outside of themselves, take responsibility for where they're going and where they are. It's vital that they find their own beauty.

They are smart conchitas and stubborn like me, Frida added. *They will make their own splendor.*

But, as their mother, I still want to give them that as well.

They have you and Jeem and your love for them no matter where we are in the world.

She was right, and I knew she was waiting for me to say that. I support them no matter where we all are, but they no longer have a "home" with their parents because their parents don't have one. I've never had to do that. I come from a family of packrats. My mother still has my room with my stuff (which I went through this past summer as part of my clearing things out). I mean she still has my "Mystery Date" game, so what can you expect? And I guess this speaks to the power of motherhood as well as the difficulty of letting go. I'm letting go of my children so they can become real adults, whether they want to or not.

Who wants to grow up? Frida wanted to know.

For months before we left, we were getting the house ready to sell. We put in a wonderful new bathroom upstairs—bright and airy, the color the same as our serene guest bedroom: "Dreamland," it was called. It was as pretty as it sounds, a turquoise of sorts, and we even included a bench in the shower because we thought that was a nice touch that we would've liked ourselves. (Why didn't I do that earlier for the kids to enjoy?) We spruced and fixed, making sure that everything in and out of the house was superb. We wanted to get the best price for our big house and lot in the best neighborhood and school district in town. We worked long and hard every day, getting all this done with workmen traipsing in and out. Of course, it took weeks longer than it was supposed to, but it finally was finished just before we were taking Bret to college in Virginia.

Two weeks after we returned from that, we were off to Jim's son Matt's wedding in Mendocino, California—our final "must" before leaving the country. Our whole blended family met there for the wonderful occasion and had a glorious long weekend together.

Jim and I had been exhausted for months and thought the house would sell right away. It didn't. A few weeks after the wedding, we decided to start packing things up anyway. Jim's book deadline was ticking, and we had to go. By the time we finally left at the end of November, we had packed and stored almost 300 boxes. (We may not have a house, but we have a lot of stuff to go in one.)

Box No. 1 is the dining room chandelier that Jim and I had bought in Montecito and shipped home 12 years before. We replaced it in July, before any prospective buyers showed up, because we didn't want to sell that chandelier with the house. Now, earlier this week, our inventive buyers complained to the Realtor that we had changed this chandelier in the last two weeks. I mean I'm flattered that they understand how faboo it is, and they certainly endow us with much more energy than we can even think about. They might've seen a *picture* of the chandelier—our house has been written up in magazines—but they never laid eyes on the actual fixture. Letting go of our house and closing it would feel better and be easier if we had been shown more good will all along. Other people we've talked with have found consolation in letting go of homes when they've liked the people they were turning their home over to.

We hoped our dog, Snapp, would be coming to France soon. Grandmother was weary, and Jim and I wanted to have him with us. It would make us happy. It would make Snapp happy. It would make Grandmother happy. We called Mother and told her we were going to bring Snapp over. I think she was doing a cheer as we hung up.

That night Jim beautifully prepared a small pork roast for dinner, with salt, pepper, garlic, and sprigs of rosemary. He peeled and chopped turnips, apples, celery, onion, pumpkin and mixed it with olive oil, poiré, salt, paprika, and cayenne. The pork roast went in first, and the vegetables were added later. The aroma seeping out of the oven was fragrant, savory, and as sweet as the glazed and golden picture when we opened up the roaster. What a beautiful meal!

It smelled like home. What is it we're grasping for after we've let go?

CHAPTER SEVENTEEN
The Enchanted Weekend

IT HAD BEEN hard to find that grounded place within myself over the last few weeks. First, I was working very hard. Then the house sold, and I felt rudderless and fearful. I had to feel the emotion, breathe it in and understand this chosen loss in a more visceral way than I had before. Finally I believed I'd been able to do it with some success. I was moving ahead.

I went shopping for Blair's birthday and filled a box with goodies for her—meats and sweets, crackers and cookies, books, bijoux, and clothes. I wrapped every gift with fuchsia, chartreuse, and purple crepe papers and tied them with red and green bows. We piled the cache of birthday booty in a carton I'd snagged from a store and mailed it through the French postal service, paying for priority delivery. This was my daughter's first birthday in 22 years that I hadn't thrown some sort of party, and it was important that our good wishes and surprises arrive on time. It was a festive cadeau! But there was one thing I'd wanted to include that I didn't have—a lore-filled gift of some sort from the land of Merlin and Viviane.

The whole time we'd been here I had been determined to see the ancient Forest of Brocéliande (also called the Forest of Paimpont), land of legends and fairies and magic, where Merlin the Sorcerer conjured up an invisible crystal castle for his great love, Viviane. Being a lover of unreality (which is reality for me), I wanted to jump into this world that troubadours and poets sang about through the Middle Ages and that has lived on in the annals of knights and chivalry. But Blair's package had to go before we got there—which we did later in the week.

Our first stop was the tiny village of St. Léry, which did not disappoint. St. Léry was pristine, with beautifully maintained houses and a glorious mansion just across the lane from the lovely 14th-century church with its smart Renaissance porch. The sky spit rain at us, but we didn't care. We were just happy to be in such a place.

The next point of interest was the Château de Comper, where Vivian the Priestess (and Fairy) was said to have been born and where she raised her son, Lancelot, who grew up to become the most gallant knight of King Arthur's Round Table. In other words, this was Sir Lancelot's boyhood home—can it get any better than that? The chateau loomed over the countryside with its great walls, tower, and mystery. The gate was closed, and we couldn't tour it, but Frida, Jim, and I peered through the gate and walked its line of walls. Viviane saw us, recognized good souls (as well as other temperamental women), and blew up a storm to say hello. There had been no wind at all—and then when we started taking photos, the gusts nearly knocked us down. I'm not kidding. It was weird.

The Lady of the Lake created such a breeze that her lagoon rippled with her breath. I told this to a French friend, and she said Viviane was jealous of Frida. (But what about me?)

Did Merlin understand what he was getting into with this powerful pixie? I think he did, but we drove on to Merlin's tomb to ask him. The earth there was red with clay, and two slabs of schist marked the spot. Not a fancy French monument like one might've suspected—just simple and natural. When I told Merlin about Viviane's gust of wind, his response was, "That was it? You got off lucky." Frida and I both remarked that Viviane had certainly found her calling within the world of enchantment, and Merlin replied that he taught her everything she knew.

After that, Jim and Frida and I ambled down the path of the Fountaine de Jouvence (Fountain of Youth), which has magical powers as well. I stuck my hand in the still, unassuming pool. Leaves were strewn across the top of it. I dripped the water across my head and neck, and Jim did the same. I certainly want all the extra power and charm I can get—not to mention any age-defying minerals that this water might hold.

The forest itself is quite serene, with towering trees and a carpet of wild flowers and leaves and such. The town of Paimpont is in the heart of it—beside a sizeable lake that looked like a shimmery, liquid skirt adorning the abbey church and square. Jim, growing impatient with all this magic, had become cranky by this point, so he didn't follow me down the main street to where I'd spied an interesting Merlin shop with lots of Arthur-related paraphernalia (as well as kitschy tourist junk). I had to have a souvenir and preferably a meaningful one. One of our dear friends from Arkansas, Greg Elliott, once told me that he knew I was half-fairy—which made Blair and Bret a quarter-fairy each. Of course, I loved that idea, since I've always longed to fly and make magic in my own right, and I happily claimed the heritage. I found the perfect fairy earrings and have worn them ever since. I also found a silver Holy Grail to hang on my necklace of icons that I've collected all over the world. Oh, rapture! I'd lacked a Grail, and since we're on this quest, it couldn't have fit more flawlessly.

After this, our last prestigious stop was the Val Sans Tour, the Valley of No Return. This is the land that Morgana, the fairy witch, forbade anyone who had been unfaithful to ever leave. Frida wouldn't even go in. The cheating Diego (whose portrait was painted on her forehead) would've had to stay behind, and Frida didn't want to take up residence there.

It was a lovely tour through tales and legends, and afterwards we arrived in Vannes in time for a wonderful dinner at a restaurant called La Gavroche. The décor, ambience, and dinner were in perfect harmony.

In fact, the whole weekend was a feast. We were invited for a Sunday double birthday lunch for our friend Alice and her and Guy's friend Jean-Pierre. The soirée was to be at Jean-Pierre and his wife

Veronique's maison. We'd met them before at Alice's and enjoyed their delightful company. I dressed up in my black leather skirt and jacket and off we went. Our contribution to the event was Mint Juleps made with Jack Daniels. Jim is a master at stirring them up, and the crowd agreed to their tastiness. Veronique set her table beautifully, with napkins and candles of blue and green, and we were presented the hugest platter of what must have been seven dozen oysters. Wow! They were right from the sea, fresh and briny. A perfectly cooked salmon came next, with lots of good wine—and finally a berry cobbler I made for dessert.

It was one of those amazing French lunches that went on for hours, with long conversations and laughs and incredible food and wine. We talked about some of the stories and press we'd been hearing—about how terribly Americans were being treated in France, not even being able to travel around the country. We were a group of two Americans, one British, and three French having a marvelous time together and grateful for our new friends. We couldn't have been welcomed more graciously.

Our world is growing larger, our lives enriched.

CHAPTER EIGHTEEN

The Light of The South

W E'D BEEN IN Auray working for seven weeks (the owners of the house had graciously allowed us to extend our stay), but now it was time to leave for the light-filled South. Our final day at our borrowed home was frightful, trying to get work finished and to face cleaning the house and packing up. It was sad yet exhilarating to be leaving. We didn't get through until late afternoon, lighting out for Nantes at 4 P.M. We would stop there to see a Matisse exhibit in the Musée des Beaux Arts. After that, we would spend a few days in Bordeaux with French friends who once lived in Little Rock!

Ultimately, though, we were bound for La Côte Basque. Not via the barbs of Truman Capote writing about New York's elite separate society in one of their favorite lairs, but instead the Southern journey of Matisse and his hideaway on the independently-minded French and Spanish Basque coast. We were ready. From here on out, it would be sun and sea, and the promise of color and light exciteboth of us. It was the promise of illuminating ourselves.

It seems too simplistic to say that Jim and I are not the same, but it's fortunate that we have such similar tastes and desires. Usually art, architecture, and the pull of a place touch us in the same ways. Even with the differences in our personalities and the ways we sometimes drive each other crazy, there is common ground in what captures us. We see something, and we may process it differently, but the same emotion is shaped.

One thing I'm learning from this trip, about art and the artists who created it, is that *art is emotion*. I didn't understand this in the same way before. I did know one of my own goals as a writer was for people *to feel something* from whatever I'd written. That was essential to me. But I didn't fully comprehend that that was the point. I thought there was an intellectual element that was full of intricacies—that historical period, technique, style, and so on made a difference in an educated perception. Now what I realize is that art—whether with paint, clay, or words—is emotion unveiled. This is the element that gives a piece cohesiveness, life, and energy.

That's what I was mulling when we arrived in Biarritz. I'd always heard about the glitz and glamour of this Côte Basque resort but had never been to this part of France. The Empress Eugénie and Napoleon III put the fishing village on the map in the 1850's, building a palace for their summer court on the sea. The beautiful people naturally followed them, for the next three-quarters of a century. Then, in the 1920s, the trendy coterie of stars and affluent stargazers moved on to Cannes and Nice.

We were happy to have our little tour of the legendary resort. Biarritz is built on the hillside with cliffs jutting down to the sea, but it's also blessed with a wide sandy beach. As the "retirement capital of France," it still exudes great appeal—though now with a touch of faded elegance. Waves crashed on rocks as we strolled above the surf and crossed a little bridge to climb the stairways of the island boulders, from which we had views of the seaside Hôtel du Palais (where the palace once stood) and, in the other direction, the "Rocher de la Vierge," the Rock of the Virgin. A statue of the Virgin Mary stands looking out to sea, and a group of terrible musicians played outside the tunnel below her. I hope she shut her ears.

It was only a few kilometers from Biarritz to St-Jean-de-Luz, which also must be stuffed with people in the summer. We hadn't made a hotel reservation. Big mistake. The Season was gearing up, the weather was bright and sunny, and vacationers were flocking to the beach like mad. We lucked out and found a room at the pleasurably modern Hotel

Hélianthal. Our room had a terrace overlooking the garden, and the bathroom and its products were fabulous. The hotel has an oceanfront spa that I would so *love* to sign up for another time.

That night we strolled over to a restaurant we'd spotted and savored amazing Serrano ham (the beginning of Basque world for us) and fish. About the latter: This was a very strange turn of events, but I, who love fish and have always looked forward to going to the beach because I could eat fresh seafood, was now finding it weird. Maybe this was from going to the French fish markets and seeing sea creatures intact with teeth and eyes. Anyway, I had gotten squeamish and didn't want to see peculiar or creepy body parts on my plate. Fillets were fine. Oysters were delicious. Nothing too fishy-tasting was okay—but suddenly fish was iffy.

After dinner, I spotted a tray of enticing after-dinner drinks delivered to a table full of men— cherry red and served in snifters with ice. With my usual insouciance, I said to the waiter, "What's that stuff they're drinking?" Thus we became devotees of the Spanish after-dinner drink, Patxaran. Oh, it is delicious, and packs a deceptive punch.

St-Jean-de-Luz was as pretty as its name, with avenues lined with plane trees, a promenade by the sea, a sandy beach, and Basque architecture, a mix of Spanish and French details. It was white, light, and silvery, with splashes of Southern color. As in Brittany, all the road signs had two names on them—French, and in this region, Basque.

Across the bay, protected by a seawall, was the village of Ciboure, where M. Matisse holed up for a while during the beginning of World War II. Ciboure was quieter and smaller than St-Jean. We saw only one hotel, but surely there were more. We had driven the few minutes over for lunch and found a row of restaurants with terraces that looked across the moored boats and blue water to St-Jean. A tethered fleet of young student sailors were being pulled behind their teacher in a bigger craft with motor—they looked like a row of baby ducks.

The next day we switched our devotion to Hemingway and drove the 30 kilometers or so to San Sebastien, Spain. It was so close and the romantic pull of Hemingway's *The Sun Also Rises* wouldn't let us resist it. San Sebastien wasn't a sleepy village as we imagined, but a city. On this Sunday afternoon we parked and promenaded along the harbor with the Spanish, as is their nature and habit, then caught the end of an orchestral concert in a gazebo on the end of a grand boulevard. We were starving and stopped at a café for lunch—tumblers of refreshing Sangria and mouth-watering tapas of various combinations of bread, anchovies, mayo, ham, roasted peppers, and croquettas, which basically resembled mashed potato hush puppies peppered with bits of ham.

As we strolled along the streets and squares of San Sebastien, we looked through the doorways of restaurants and bars. Platters of tapas lined up on the counters scented the air with their savory aromas. The crush of lunch had ended with cigarette butts stomped on the floors. But people still sat in the afternoon sun eating and drinking, while others performed their social sauntering. We stumbled upon a trio of jazz accordionists playing for a crowd. Jim sketched the scene while I poked around the colossal and attractive Constitution Square.

For me, there was no trace of Hemingway except perhaps in the spirit of a Spanish Sunday afternoon in the separatist Basque Country. I suppose you could say that "La Côte Basque" society that Mr. Capote captured in his own inimitable way was just as separatist as the Spanish coast it was named for. And the modern flocks of beautiful people who adored and then spurned him were just as fickle as the glamorous hordes who moved on to the Côte d'Azur.

CHAPTER NINETEEN
The Healing Land

TODAY WE STOPPED to be healed. "I said *healed*, brothers and sisters," as the inimitable rooster Foghorn Leghorn might say. Having left St-Jean-de-Luz, we zipped along the main highway, but a short 25 kilometers away was Lourdes. It had nothing to do with Matisse, though he might well have made the trip himself. Who wouldn't want to be healed? And when would we have another opportunity like this—to wash ourselves in restorative waters that might take our troubles away? We aren't Roman Catholics, but who cares? I was happy to take a shot at my own miracle, and I'd been working on healing myself for years through various spiritual endeavors. I was ready, willing, and open to the experience. Jim veered to the exit like a man on a mission.

The countryside was fresh and green with sheep and horses grazing in the pastures. The snow-capped peaks of the Pyrénées loomed above this little burg of 15,000 people—a town with 40,000 hotel rooms! What? I had no idea. Lourdes' fame is well known, of course, and I had seen the Hollywood movie *The Song of Bernadette*, with Jennifer Jones. But who knew this place attracted some five million visitors a year—the most-visited Christian pilgrimage site in the world?

The setting of the town is charming, though Bernadette changed its ambience forever with her visions of the Virgin Mary and her uncovering of the miraculous spring that soon became renowned for its healing powers. As we strode up the Esplanade des Processions, banners waved and life-sized cutouts of crippled people greeted us. Jim said it was like being at Disney World, and he certainly had a point, with the castle-like Basilique du Rosaire with its enormous gold crown at the end of the walk. We circled around to the famous grotto where we could see the curative spring bubbling forth. Lining a rock wall were faucets that conveniently delivered the hallowed waters. We washed our hands and dabbed our faces with it. I sprinkled it on my head and suggested that Jim do the same. I was hoping that even negative thought patterns could be mended.

Afterwards, we lit a huge candle for our loved ones and said prayers. I also bought a few smaller candles to take with us for our own private ritual. As you might imagine, souvenir shops lined the narrow rues, and I bought plenty of medals and trinkets. I knew a lot of people who could use a little healing, and this seemed to be the mother lode of it.

After Lourdes, our drive across southwestern France from the Basque country to the Languedoc-Roussillon was sublime. The Pyrénées rose on our right, and castles and hilltop towns dotted the lush countryside. Toulouse had been our destination, but there were no rooms at any inn so we opted for Carcassonne as a base. The wonder of Carcassonne is the enormous and beautifully restored fortress, the cité.

We arrived in the dark and found the tight gateway of the Porte Narbonnaise, the only place a car can get through; unless you're staying there, you must park outside. The walled town was quiet and the cobblestone streets tiny. We prefer arriving in a town when we can still see, but we easily found our Best Western hotel, the Du Donjon, that I believe had once been an orphanage. We had a nice big room looking onto the garden. We would be there three days—which meant we had found a home again.

Once we were settled, we began our evening stroll, discovering in the process an adorable restaurant for dinner. Their specialty was cassoulet, that wonderful casserole of white beans, duck or goose, sausage, and maybe even pork—a dish that's native to the area. We paired it with a good red wine, and earthy comfort was ours once again.

To our great dismay, we had missed the Academy Awards the night before. We're movie buffs, and at home the Oscars were a must in our house. But this year—for the first time I could remember—I hadn't seen a single one of the movies nominated for Best Picture. That still didn't take away my desire to watch the Oscar spectacle. I mean whose dresses were good, whose were bad, and the same for the speeches and the host's jokes.

When we returned to our room after dinner, we found a shortened version of the broadcast on French TV. Even though it had been dubbed in French, it satisfied our craving. We went to bed happy.

The next day we made the trip back to the Midi-Pyrénées and Toulouse, which is a city of 650,000 with 110,000 university students. It's known as La Ville Rose because of the millions of pink bricks that radiate from its buildings. As the sun changes positions in the sky, the color of Toulouse changes to pinks, oranges, roses, and reds. Toulouse, the lively home of many industries, was also the home of Madame Matisse and her family—with whom the young couple had stayed for a while. That's why we were there.

We chose a café on the Place du Capitole for lunch and watched as the market closed down in the square and people hurriedly walked by or stopped and ordered a meal. We were there long enough to watch a demonstration in front of the city hall that seemed to be about homeless people. I don't think we were included in their noisy appeal.

Spotting a Virgin Megastore (definitely a mecca for me), we went in and purchased the third season of "The Sopranos" (despite my entreaties to friends and family back home, no one had sent it to us) and the fourth season of "Sex and the City." The comfort of good television (or even mindless TV, if it's the right show) watched on a laptop computer cannot be discounted when you're constantly on the move.

Having read about the famous violet candy of Toulouse, I had to try some. We found it in a shop around the corner. I chit-chatted with the clerk, who told me the elderly madame in the back wrapping huge chocolate fish in green foil was the proprietor and master chocolatier. The shop was a riot of colorful foils and candies in various spring-themed shapes.

Jim had begun the day a little cranky and now, exasperated by my distractions of candy, pop culture, and especially *shopping*, he had finally revved up to an ornery growl. After a spat, we split up—he to find the Matisse connections and me to wander the rues and peruse some shops. There were lots of nice ones, and roaming alone with no purpose was dandy. We both needed some space. He chased Matisse and I enjoyed exploring a part of the old city—a cornucopia of pink buildings that surely held an energy that the young artist responded to. I bought nothing after the DVDs and beautiful candied violets, but had a lovely afternoon just walking and looking. I ended at a café for a coffee and to read my novel. It was divine.

Our drive back to Carcassone was enhanced by vineyards, villages, and chateaux. I read to Jim about the Cathar country and the Corbiere (whose wine we love), as well as the village of Limoux with its carnival and its sparkling wine called Blanquette. Southwestern France was grabbing us, and we were ready to be grabbed.

That night and the next we ordered cassoulet again. White beans and goose, sausage and pork, bubbling hot and crispy brown on top with a bottle of red wine from the region—it was all delicious and very reassuring. We felt the country healing us again and again.

CHAPTER TWENTY

Coup de Foudre

"**D**ON'T LOOK," I said, "but this is such an incredible view. Really amazing...but *don't look!*"

Jim was winding around the dazzling and dramatic cliffs of the Costa Brava with villages nestled among mountains that fanned and dropped to the sea. As the road climbed higher and higher, the view got better and better, but it was one of those terrifying drives, spectacular and scary with no railing along the way. If I'd been steering the car and chanced a glance, I'd have swooned with vertigo. One slip and, well, you could be Princess Grace with or without stroke.

We'd made a several-day detour to Barcelona to visit Jim's son and daughter-in-law, David and Erin, who were vacationing there. Now we were on the coast road from Spain back to France, a trip that plays games with gravity. After the cliffs fling us mortals into the sky, the terraced vineyards quilting the mountains bring us back to earth. A fresh Mediterranean breeze blows seduction from shore to shore, while the hum of Catalonian history reverberates in the cicadas' songs. It was an electrifying experience of a part of the world that neither of us had ever seen before.

To my horror, Jim stole a few peeks. But view or not, he was already thrilled—we were finally headed to Collioure. This French seaside village was just up the road and had been much on Jim's mind since we left Belle Isle. Yes, besides charm and beauty, I'm talking a major artistic moment in the life of Matisse. The great painter saw (noticed, experienced, realized, understood, visualized, recognized) the light of the South, as in the gospel song. To add to the excitement, we had also imagined the area as a place we might like to live. We'd been told that Southwestern France wasn't as heavily traveled or as touristy as Provence, though it was just as beautiful (and less expensive). Not to mention that I had long envisioned living in a fishing village, though that wish predated my current feelings about fish.

We'd read and heard about the Côte Vermeille, which also includes Banyuls-sur-Mer, a charming seaside village that's also famous for its regional wine. The next village, Port Vendres, was also dandy—but neither held a candle to Collioure. We drove in through more mountains and vineyards, finally descending to the intimate bay with its citadel and castle floating on the Mediterranean. Narrow rues running up to the views and down to the water provided a piping of cobblestone that outlined the old village. Townhouses of many colors stood one after another. The energy was relaxed, but also *vibrant*. Between the sounds and the smells of the sea and the frying garlic everywhere, we immediately felt as happy as cooing doves at twilight.

Soon we were thinking that we might want to live *here*, an idea that hadn't seriously struck us anywhere since Paris (although we felt a slight tug at St-Jean-de-Luz). Collioure is a town of art and artists, and this began back in 1905 with M. Matisse. Back then the houses were not brightly colored, but were dull and drab and the bay smelled of anchovy innards. But even so, the setting was no less than splendid.

Even with the sky spitting rain, our enthusiasm was not dampened. Our first day there we wandered and looked, seeing what we could see. After lunch on the waterfront, we dropped by a gallery that had caught our eye and curiosity. The owner, Carol Watanabe, had expressed her joy of Collioure in a colorful sign in front of her place—it was all about "finding her solace." Why not? We were looking for ours as well. The fact that she felt so was a good omen, and inclined us to want to speak with her. I could tell from the sign that she was probably an American. The door was open, and we walked in.

Manning the gallery was an English woman and artist named Tessa Harris, who told us she'd lived in Collioure the past year but had stayed with a friend in the nearby Pyrenees for several years before that. We liked Tessa right away, as well as her painting of a nearby square. During our conversation, we told her we might want to find a flat or house here. As we were leaving, she remembered two apartments that had been available, and asked if we would like her to call the owner, Gerard, and inquire. Well yes, we would. She got him on the phone, and we immediately left to meet him. Could our luck really be this good?

Gerard's lovely old building was on the other side of the village away from the heavy tourist traffic. That could be nice, we thought, since in July and August the town is packed with vacationers. Also, Gerard's apartments had just been beautifully renovated and air conditioned. He lived on the first floor. The second-floor flat was huge, with spacious rooms where we could work, live, and have visitors. The building even had an elevator, which was in and of itself a miracle. It boded well for us and would be good for my mother when she came to visit.

The only problem—the flat was unfurnished. With all the furniture we now had in storage in Arkansas, how could we commit to buying more to live here? We'd just taken a house apart. We didn't want to put one together again—and we certainly weren't ready to ship our belongings over and then have to wrestle with that added baggage.

The third-floor flat was a cool and nicely decorated loft. We loved the space and the view from a small balcony. But it was much smaller, and Gerard had in mind for it to be rented throughout the season on a weekly basis—which meant much more money than the larger unfurnished one.

These spaces had landed in our laps within 24 hours, but what to do? Neither one fit us perfectly, but as the French say, we had suffered a "coup de foudre," a lightning bolt of love. That night we talked to Blair and Bret but couldn't get Mother on the phone, and the next morning Jim went out sketching. He was deliriously happy. It was shining in his eyes and his body was lighter. The beauty of Collioure is radiant in its art and energy and sea and sky and vineyard-covered hills, and he was reflecting it.

That evening we had tapas for dinner at a local hangout called Le Zouave. The fresh garlic was pungent and pervasive in all our tastes of this and that, including fantastic calamari and fresh tomato puréed with the ail and dolloped on good bread. Collioure is in Catalan country, which is the collision of France and Spain on the opposite coast from the Basque side. Catalonia reaches as far south as Barcelona and north past Perpignan. The Spanish influence is felt in all the traditions, as well as in the food and the look of the people.

The next morning we met Tessa for coffee at a café near the sea. Gerard and a friend were sitting a few rows away, and they soon joined us. Gerard's friend, Pamela, was Canadian and was preparing to return home after traveling for some months in France with not a lot of money. We talked as travelers often do about how much energy it takes to be open to see the world around you, to process what you find. Again, we notice that the people you meet wandering the world are amazing, interesting, usually open and adventurous. We impressed Gerard once more with our interest in his flat and then strolled a few blocks away to take a look at Tessa's home. After meeting our generous new friend a mere two days before, she offered to loan us her furniture that was stored in the Pyrenees. We only had to retrieve it.

Late that afternoon, I finally reached my mother. She sounded excellent, which made me happy. I told her about the flat and its elevator that would be a big advantage for her when she came to visit this summer. She could walk the few steps to the sea and sit and look out, with her eyes and heart, at the blue Mediterranean. My family had always been drawn to the water, and Mother found joy and peace in gazing at a river, lake, or ocean. She would also love the spectacular yet frightening Costa Brava drive, with me imploring Jim to keep his eyes on the wheel. We talked of my children and laughed and laughed. This was the last conversation I would ever have with her.

CHAPTER TWENTY-ONE
As Dreamers Do

TESSA HAD ENCOURAGED us to see a real estate agent to learn more about the rental market here before we made a commitment to Gerard. We were already enthralled with both of Gerard's apartments, though neither fit us perfectly. Frankly, we didn't want to mess with a real estate agent, so we were going to blow it off. But Tessa's concern got the best of us. Finding a place for the summer was what we'd planned on arranging all along, but where? After living in the same house for 13 years and hating in some ways to give it up, we suddenly felt hesitant about making a commitment for a few months. Traveling all the time is hard, but one of the great points about it is seeing and experiencing new places constantly. There's no time to get bored. Choosing a place to stay for several months loomed large in our minds.

When we walked into the Real Estate office, the agent behind the desk was a petite woman with coiffured dark hair who was dressed expensively in Italian boots that were on the side of "too much"—a style that many French women prefer. We told her what we were doing and what we were looking for. She checked her books and came up with a two-bedroom/two-bath flat in merely Jim's favorite building in Collioure. It's next to the church and looks like a pink castle with green shutters the color of grass and a huge terrace that would hold quite a fête for tinkling cocktails and a view of the sea. Not bad, as M. Malric of the Hotel Saint Germain would say. The price? Well, not in our league, but I asked The Real Estate Agent to take a look at our website and to ask the owner to view it as well. She didn't understand why.

As I was explaining how some people were helping this valiant quest of ours by providing accommodations, she interrupted me. "Pardon me," she said, "but you are a dreamer. This is business to these people."

Jim rushed to my defense by jumping in and telling her that others had seen this *as* business. I caught my breath and added, "This is marketing."

But the damage was done. My bubble was burst. Me? A dreamer? It was true, of course, but also a stake in my heart. This has been one of my strengths and weaknesses my entire life—being a dreamer. My glory and my torture. My creativity and art, and gulp, the real world that I preferred not living in as compared to the one in my head. Oh, when I get the Hollywood Ending, I will show all the naysayers—including The Real Estate Agent. When I've persevered and stuck it out and I am the hero and all good things come to me, I will still be a dreamer, but this time with results. Collioure is known for its artists. Don't I fit in here? We told her we'd call her later that afternoon (like that was ever going to happen) and fled for the Hotel Les Templiers, where we were staying, and its proprietor, Monsieur Jojo Pous.

M. Pous's family had supported a dreamer or two who had done quite well—Matisse, Picasso, Dufy, Derain, among many others. I only wish I'd thought of pointing that out. Part of what The Real Estate Agent should be marketing in Collioure is that it is a town of artists. Les Templiers proves it.

Les Templiers is a bastion of Pous family energy, with their and Collioure's history covering the walls. The bar is the perfect saloon, and the hotel is charming and comfortable like you were a guest at a gigantic weekend party in a shabby chic house. M. Pous's children are now in charge. His daughter, Mané, runs the excellent restaurant and son Jean-Michel runs the hotel. When M. Pous walked in the door, I realized I'd seen him around town. He's now 74, with white hair and bright eyes and a personality to match. He speaks little English, so his fabulous employee Veronique interpreted for us.

His grandmother, Marie, started the business in the late 1800s with a bar called the Café des Sports. His parents built the place up, attracting all the passing artists. Eventually they came here just to spend time, drink and hang out, and feel at home and part of the Pous family. The Pouses and their bar (and later hotel) provided a haven of support and good spirit for any artists who walked in their door. In turn, the artists gave the Pous family some 2,000 paintings over the years—each one a part of his life, M. Pous said. Paintings and drawings covered every inch of the hotel and bar walls—so many they cannot all be hung—but the priceless art had to be taken down 25 years ago when three Picasso drawings were stolen. The Pouses and the dreamers were friends and compatriots in both art and commerce. M. Pous told us he owned a book of art that artists like those named above had filled with their work and signed. If we wanted, we could see it!

The next day, Mané Pous set the hallowed book down in front of us—and left us alone with it for an hour or two. At our fingertips were original works by Matisse, Picasso, Dufy, Maillol, and many more. We turned the pages: One after another, these pictures dazzled us— interesting, inspired, beautiful, provocative, complex, simple, wild, tame, bursting with color, elegantly black and white. Whether drawing or painting, each was a unique expression of the masters and other artists who had wanted to honor the Pouses, their Café des Sports, and then Les Templiers. In the pages of this book are life and art and history—the visions, memories, and imaginations of the artists who were touched by the light of Collioure and their happy relationship with this Catalan family. The introduction, although we couldn't read it all, contemplated the Joyous Spirit of all of the above.

More and more, we were dying to be in Collioure this summer, to spend time at Les Templiers, to be part of the Joyous Spirit that so many artists had experienced before us. After returning The Book to Mané, we stayed for a delicious lunch. We felt at home there. I knew I could actually learn French in the bar!

But we still hadn't made the commitment, because our wishy-washiness was a nagging demon that tortured us with thoughts and images of all the places in the South of France that we hadn't yet seen. Was there some better place? Would someone say he or she had a house that we could use? Maybe this crazy Iraq war would actually benefit us, because fewer Americans would be coming to France. More properties would be available, more chances for a lagniappe to fall in our laps. (I like my options open as long as possible.)

That afternoon we found out Gerard had returned to his other house in Mirepoix, and we hadn't given him our answer. Our hearts now told us it should be yes—definitely—without any of that devilish ambiguity. It would have to be the unfurnished flat—it was a good deal and space—even though the thought of equipping it gave me a feeling of dread. It was an energy-sapping job I really didn't want—much less the expense. We looked at another apartment that was too small, and I bought a straw purse that matched my new chartreuse sandals. Now I was totally accessorized for Collioure. Was this a sign?

On our way back to the hotel, I stuck my hand in the Mediterranean, which was frigid. Jim went on to do laundry and I tried on beachy clothes. How horrible! I looked so bad I went right to a snack bar and bought some Catalan fondant treats called Rousquilles, ate four of them, and went to our room and climbed in bed.

Jim returned from the laundromat with bad news. Gerard had called. He'd offered the flat to someone else—obviously someone with fewer issues than us. We had let our chance in Collioure slip through our fingers.

CHAPTER TWENTY-TWO
Blow The House Down

W E LEFT COLLIOURE feeling like fools. We did manage to have lunch in Perpignan, which was a miracle. With our impeccable timing, we usually arrive at a restaurant right after they've stopped serving the midday meal.

Today we were off to the Camargue. On our six-week trip to France a few years back I'd wanted to stop there but we couldn't fit it in. Now we were making a special visit, even though the Camargue had nothing whatsoever to do with Monsieur Matisse. It was, at least, on the *way* to more Matisse country—Cassis, St. Tropez, and Nice. Driving along La Grand Motte was like driving the Gulf Coast of Florida—heavy traffic, high rise hotels, azure oceans and skies. We knew we'd crossed over and were in French cowboy country when we started seeing one stable after another, with the white Camargue horses pacing their corrals, or saddled up with people taking trail rides. These horses have an Arabian look about them, and the Camargue resembles the American plains— wide, flat, and dusty, though the French West has one thing its American counterpart does not have, and that is tons and tons of salt. (Not to mention the flamingoes.)

We arrived at Stes-Maries-de-la-Mer, a seaside village named for three Marys of Jesus fame—Magdalene, Jacobea (the Virgin Mary's sister), and Salome (mother of apostles James and John)—who were said to have been set adrift in a boat on the Mediterranean after the Crucifixion. They were supposed to have ended up here along with their servant, Sara. When you spend time around the Mediterranean, you find Biblical characters popping up all over the place. This sea isn't as big as you might think. Either that or they really made tracks to get to all the places that claim them.

There are two festivals for the Marys in May and October that I would love to attend, but the one I'm really dying to hit is the one in May—because that's when gypsies from around the world come to pay their respects to their patron saint, the aforementioned Sara. There are bullfights, horse races, and flamenco dancing. And with all the gypsies, what a spectacle! Jim seemed less enthusiastic than I.

For the next few nights we were staying at the Hotel de Cacheral, a Camarguais version of the Ponderosa. The owner's house and the bunk houses where the guests stay were whitewashed and looked out on salt marshes where hundreds of pink flamingoes made a surreal installation in the deep blue of the sky and water below them. Jim and I walked out to the marsh to get a better look at the birds, a herd of white horses being fed with hay, and the Camarguais black cattle with horns. We signed up for a trail ride the next morning.

After dark we went into the village and ate a wonderful dinner of taureau steak (the black cattle). The beef was tasty and had a tang of the wild. Later, in our hotel room, we lit the three candles we'd been carrying with us since Lourdes. We said prayers for our loved ones and went to bed. That night the wind blew so hard it rattled the walls. I heard the roar, though slept fine. But Jim was awake almost all night. He said he thought it was going to blow the house down.

It was 7:15 A.M. when our phone rang. My brother, Blair, was calling to tell me that he had some really horrible news: Our mother was dead. He gave me the details, which I didn't really hear. I guess the words went in my ears—the syllables, the phrases—but there was no comprehension. I simply couldn't believe it. *My mother was dead.*

When my father died at 42—almost 34 years before—it was also an awful trauma. His death was an accident—he was scuba diving with a new contraption that was all the rage, an air compressor that floated on top of the water with hose and mask connected to the diver underneath. He was spear fishing, and we believe he was after a big one. He went down too far, the compressor turned over, and he came up too fast. It was a Sunday afternoon, and our neighbor called to tell us that he'd heard Daddy had died at the lake. I was 15 at the time and paced the family room wringing my hands, worrying about the teenage flak that had been flying between my father and me. My mother, Bobbye Ann, said, "Maybe it's not true." But in a few minutes we saw our minister pulling into the driveway.

That had been a Sunday afternoon in August. This was an April Sunday morning—for me; a Saturday night for Mother—a week before my birthday and what would've been my parents' 51st wedding anniversary, if they had lived. We didn't expect this phone call. Does one ever? Even when my younger brother, Brent, died in 1990 of AIDS, we didn't expect his death at the time that it came. I hoped beyond hope that his body could find a way to beat this illness and live. Today he probably could have, but not then.

Bobbye Ann had high blood pressure and high cholesterol, and she did need to lose weight, but she lived a busy, vital life and looked beautiful. People never thought she was as old as her 74 years. She had always told us she would die young. Her father and brother passed on in their 50s with heart attacks, and her father's mother, her favorite grandmother with whom she'd spent lots of time, did too. Of the others, my mother's mother was still living at 96, and *her* mother had lived into her 90's as well. Bobbye Ann always told us her mother would outlive her, but we just pooh-poohed. We thought she had the long-life genes. Did she know, or had she created her own reality? Perhaps it was simply time for her soul to go. The time she'd contracted for when she came into this life was done. Mission accomplished. All her lessons learned.

A doctor friend of mine thought death was random, but then he killed himself. There was no randomness to that.

Basically, what I found out later was that Mother had called Blair and told him she didn't feel well. She had a headache (which she never had) and was sweating. He offered to take her to the ER, but she said no and took an aspirin. When he talked with her a short time later, she said she felt better. Then he heard her hit the floor. The paramedics said she probably died instantly. A couple of doctor friends of ours said it sounded like an aneurysm.

Jim had been right about the raging wind that howled the night before. It *had* blown our house down.

CHAPTER TWENTY-THREE
Abandonment

I CALLED MY older daughter, Blair, and gave her the terrible news. I couldn't reach her sister, Bret. Then I phoned a couple of old friends who'd known Mother well, and with whom I could voice my disbelief, horror, and pain.

We spent the rest of the morning trying to get a flight home on Delta Airlines. We already had return tickets for May (which we actually hadn't planned to use). Now they were our way home for my mother's funeral. Marseille was the closest airport, so we would drive there, leave the car, and fly to Paris. But we couldn't get there in time to get out of Paris that day, so we would spend the night at our wonderful Hotel Saint Germain (the staff there immediately offered help) and leave Paris the next. The staff of the Hotel de Cacheral outside of Stes-Maries-de-la-Mer also were great. They immediately said we could leave all of our things there, and helped us move them to the owner's house in a guest room, so they would be safe until we returned to claim them.

In Little Rock, some of our dearest friends were at the airport to greet us. We'd been nomads only a little over four months, and we had enjoyed it; but it was wonderful to be with people we knew and cared about and who cared deeply about us. Jim and I drove on to Batesville, where Blair and Bret were already at Grandmother's house—the house where I grew up, the house that my mother and father had hired an architect to plan and build. My mother had made sure the builders did their absolute best work in creating the house she wanted. We moved in when I was seven years old.

It is a fine and well-thought-out house that my mother filled with tasteful antiques that she searched the countryside for, and that she infused with savory and sweet smells from the delicious meals she cooked every day. The food was all homemade. No cookies were bought in packages at the store. Ours were baked in her oven along with her pies. Her strawberry preserves and blackberry jams were perfectly jelled. She made me some of my prettiest dresses until I became too much of a know-it-all. She washed and curled my long hair so I looked the proper and well-kept little girl. We picnicked and played croquet and badminton in our yard, drove to the lake every weekend to swim, ski, and play.

My parents let us be wild and free—which was quite a gift for us, though not for the other people at the restaurants, whom we terrorized, and the people whose yards we ran through while we played. Mother drove us to glaciers in Colorado and villages in old Mexico. She taught me the courage and fearlessness that I'm not sure she knew she had. She became a widow at age 41 with three teenagers to raise and didn't run away. She potty-trained my children. What else can I say? She was the President of her Scotch-Irish clan, Clan McAlister, and was proud of her name. She was a smart businesswoman who managed her money and investments well, and what we heard over and over again in Batesville was that she helped people constantly and didn't expect acclaim.

Bobbye Ann lived at 1775 Maple for 42 years. That house lived and breathed her. And now, without her, it felt positively empty—even with all of us there.

* * *

I SLEPT VERY little for days. There was too much awful business to attend to, decisions to make, and I wanted this memorial for my mother to be personal and dear, a celebration of her life. But I was wrung out. My body clock was whacked, and my brain wouldn't work. I didn't recognize people I'd known my whole life.

We were excited to see our pets, Snapp and Cleo, but they had mixed reactions to us. Before this, whenever we went away on a trip, feline Cleo usually acted mad when we returned. This time she couldn't have been friendlier. Snapp the dog, who was usually beside himself when we came home, snubbed us, which of course hurt our feelings. We may have left, but we hadn't abandoned him. Had we? In truth, I think all the children, whether human or animal, felt alike. We hadn't given them up, but we'd left all the same.

Mother's funeral was grand with the McAlister tartan up on display, flowers cascading everywhere, and the church I'd grown up in filled with friends and family. It felt *intime* as I stood up to deliver the eulogy I so wanted to give to honor my mother publicly.

I think the desire to please your parents never goes away, and it wasn't always easy to please Bobbye. She'd devoted herself to us when we were young children and dealt as best she could with the young widowhood she was forced into when my father suddenly died. But it was tough, and she didn't get support from people who should have supported her. Difficult years followed. When my younger brother Brent died, that was another terrible loss for us. Mother could've become bitter, but she grew and mellowed, and she and I forged a different relationship. She appreciated my caring heart, work, and hardships with my own children. She expanded and evolved to support gay rights and causes, when it had once been problematical for her to accept that her son was gay and died of AIDS. Her liberal Democratic political views were an area we always bonded in, and as I had matured and she'd gotten older, we'd each seen the other more clearly and forgiven old hurts.

She had been sad for Jim and me to leave for Europe. She'd valued our not being far away. Did she feel abandoned as well? I hate it that my mother was sad and lonely, though I believe this is partially a function of age or, at the other end of the spectrum, can happen any time throughout life. I suspect she felt this way more often than I would like to admit or think about.

We were in Arkansas for almost two weeks, and then it was time to return to chasing Matisse. I still felt exhausted and was on the verge of freaking out. I had to leave much undone at my beloved mother's house, and the thought of dismantling it was almost more than I could bear. In fact, the two homes I'd once had and adored would be gone in less than a year. This is major psychological trauma in anyone's book—on top of the fact that My Mother Is Dead and never got to go to France and enjoy the nice life we had there. Even so, I believe she is bathed in the light of God, surrounded by joy, peace, and her loved ones.

Friend Patti drove us to the airport in her newly-restored 1964 1/2 Mustang convertible. Otherwise, I would've wept and wept. But the wind blowing through my hair in that cool car was a tonic. It was difficult to leave and hard to stay in Arkansas. France reclaimed me.

Life goes on. The world evolves, and so do we with love and laughter and new beginnings. But life also stops. It will never be the same again, and this hits me at the oddest moments. At such times, I feel the loss of Mother empty in me. It can never be refilled. I am sorrow. I am like my children and pets: My mother did not abandon me, but I am abandoned as well.

CHAPTER TWENTY-FOUR

Shedding My Skin

WE ARRIVED IN Marseille not knowing where we would spend the night. The Hotel de Cacharel—where we'd left all the belongings we'd been hauling all over France— was full. I called our next stop along the way—the Mahogany Hotel de la Plage in Cassis. I have never been more delighted than when the helpful clerk told me they had a garden room. Jim, being a dear and a trouper, would drive back to the Cacharel the next day to retrieve our stuff. The lovely Cassis—where Matisse basked in the light and Winston Churchilll learned how to paint—was only 30 minutes from Marseille, smack dab on the Mediterranean.

When we arrived, we were shown to a large and lovely room in deep Provencal red and gold, with brick floors, lovely products, and a bath. Oooh la la! The Mahogany was directly across the street from a wonderful beach, and the view was magnificent. That night we had an elegant dinner at the Jardin d'Emile restaurant next door. I savored a delicious vegetable flan and fish, while Jim relished hot chevre and lamb with artichoke hearts.

It was Easter, one of Mother's favorite holidays. Mine too. Should we have stayed and enjoyed the holiday with our family? I don't know. Bret had left for Virginia. She'd already missed a week of school. Blair would've been happy to spend more time with us, and it would've been nice to be with my brother and his family. But Jim and I both felt pressure to get back and continue our adventure and journey. He had a book to write, a deadline to meet, and we were already behind.

The next day, while Jim drove back to the Camargue, I slept late and then packed up our suitcases to move to a room with a view of the sea. Our garden chambre was luscious, and larger than the new one, but it didn't have the Mediterranean view—water in hues of milky to deep emerald green by the shore, and as the liquid became deeper, ponds of deep purple spread over the cobalt sea. I walked to the village and bought a bottle of Champagne, which we drank on our balcony when Jim got back. The sun was setting, and the sea reflected the copper of the mountain it lapped up to. The moment was serene.

We stayed in Cassis several days, tracing M. Matisse's footsteps and generally getting to know the lovely town. But mostly we rested, exhausted as we were after our long ordeal. To my mind, the most important—and perhaps symbolic—event of our time in Cassis happened on the beach.

One morning we were sitting on our balcony enjoying breakfast and observing the topless sunbathers at the beach. Jim asked me if American women were the only ones who don't spend part of their adult public lives with uncovered breasts. He brought up all the *National Geographic* photos of African and other native women who don't clothe their bosoms. Good point, I thought, and who cares about their bare breasts, anyway? Another question arises: Do all European women disrobe their chests for sunbathing? I don't know. I doubt the Spanish-influenced cultures engage in this tradition. Too many macho men would have heart failure, kill someone, or both.

But the French women sunbathe—and sunbathe *topless*—no matter how fat or thin they are—or old or young, pregnant, or for any other reason that would prevent an American from doing it, at least as far as I can tell. French women accept their body-types publicly, and they take pleasure in emancipating their breasts while lying in the hot sun.

Listen, sisters, I don't blame them. It feels happy and free to have sunbeams warming your usually bound and covered chest. It's not even bold behavior here. Almost all French women do it with their husbands and children, grandchildren, boyfriends, fathers, sons, and brothers—anyone—around. It is an established piece of culture that no one even thinks about. It's not sexual. You don't see a bunch of men with their tongues hanging out, staring, or making lewd remarks. Topless sunbathers are not slutty, forward, or unusual. They're remarkably status quo. French men see bare breasts, boobs, titties, knockers, headlights, honkers, hooters, jugs—whatever you want to call them—all the time at the beach and pool. So?

Anyway, the sun was hot and we put on our suits and walked over to the beach, found a spot on the rocks, and laid out our towels. As I slathered on my sunscreen, my skin came off in rolls. *I was actually shedding my skin!* Was my body telling me something that my mind hadn't yet registered? Was that late-April date important in some way? I decided it was—that shedding old skin was a very good thing!

So I peeled my top down. My suit was a one-piece, and after a few minutes I didn't even care that my own breasts were basking naked in the sun with multitudes around. Unless I did this many years ago, this is the first time I recall being topless at a French beach. We've foregone the coast every other time we've been here. Frankly, I don't remember, but Jim liked the fact that I bared myself like all the other women. I took this as a compliment, since I personally wished I weighed about 20 pounds less.

Swimming was not on my agenda. The water was icy, and I'm not a cold-water girl. So even though the sun was searing, I walked in up to my hips once and retreated to the shore. While Jim sketched, I stretched back on the pebbles, listened to the sea, and looked at the sky.

Thoughts of my mother drift in with the tide. The feelings wash over me, yet her death does not seem real. I think I have more skin to shed.

CHAPTER TWENTY-FIVE

The View From On High

ONCE MATISSE MADE enough money, he gave up Collioure for glitzier Nice. Although it took me several days to appreciate and understand the textures of this big Mediterranean city, with all its Italian flavors, I eventually liked it so much that I hated to leave. The Hotel Le Grimaldi was our home while we explored M. Matisse's haunts in and around this part of the Cote d'Azur. Such a lovely hotel—it was a great comfort as well as a pleasure to be their guest.

I could fill an entire book with the hedonistic pleasures of Nice. One night we promenaded to the famous Hotel Negresco for a drink. The Negresco is pink and fabulous from the outside, and the bar is classic clubby with handsome polished wood and tailored, rich fabrics, beautiful people sitting around, all the women dripping in jewels. We sat down, and I slung my jacket over my chair like this was nothing for me. When the very proper waiter leaned over to quietly greet us, Jim ordered us Gin Fizzes. The cool refreshments were perfectly made and elegantly delivered with petite bowls of crunchy snacks.

The problem was, we were bored. If one can afford a luxurious five-star hotel, does this mean that he or she is dull? Or is the level of pretension such that life has ebbed away? Or was it just the evening?

Later I danced down the Promenade des Anglais before a group of musicians playing away with a beat that my body wanted to move to. Eventually, we made our way down the boulevard to the Colline de

Chateau, which has one of the most stunning views of Nice's half-moon bay, lights sparkling in the twilight, and the Mediterranean mirroring this delight. We stopped in at the Hotel La Perouse right below it for another libation, another Gin Fizz to be exact. We were led to the garden bar and restaurant (good thing, since it was a labyrinth to get there), and we watched as the waiter picked a lemon from the tree for our drinks. This was charming as all get out, as were the hidden garden and romantic pool.

The Hotel La Perouse was the vantage point from which Raoul Dufy, Matisse's contemporary (and secret nemesis), painted his stunning views of Nice's Baie des Anges. Matisse staked out higher ground, living for many years in a high-rise apartment building in the old Roman town of Cimiez, a garden in the clouds above Nice. The Romans knew how to choose all the best spots, and Cimiez is one of them. It was a city of an estimated 20,000 residents that has a most magnificent view and ethereal air. There's something about it that exudes civilized serenity. I can only imagine what it must have been like in 300 B.C. without apartments like the Hotel Regina, where Matisse lived the last years of his life—although, again, what an inspiring view and gentle atmosphere he found before his death in 1954.

One day Jim and I drove into the hills looking for the Regina and the nearby Musée Matisse. The latter is a palatial and beautiful rose-colored Italian villa with grand *trompe l'oeil* shutters and other architectural accoutrements that are so realistic it takes some time to notice they're not genuine. The grounds are ample, as they should be for a house/museum of this scale, set in a park with a small amphitheatre where jazz concerts are held. The paths through it have names of the greats like Duke Ellington and Miles Davis. What a blend of time and space, talent and state—French art, Italian style, and American jazz in the palm of ancient history.

The collection inside the impressive villa was—God forbid I say this—okay but not stunning. Oh, what was there was perfectly nice, but evidently Matisse sold most of his paintings and enjoyed the income. I guess there wasn't much left for him to give away, and many of the pieces were donated by Madame Matisse, who hadn't even lived with him for years when he died. Some years before, Madame Matisse's nurse, Lydia Delectorskya, evolved into the painter's model, then assistant, and finally companion. Lydia was his mate for more than a decade before he died.

I don't know if the Matisses divorced, but I thought it was generous of Madame Matisse to contribute her husband's work to his museum to which he didn't leave much himself. Especially since she apparently wasn't too happy about the whole Lydia situation, and why would she be? I can imagine that M. Matisse had used up his wife's energy and patience and needed some fresh adoration and blood. I can see both points of view. Really, I can. I was most interested in the personal items of Matisse, many of which you see in his paintings—a pitcher and table and chairs, Moroccan wall hangings, and the like.

At the end of the street is the Monastere Franciscan, whose gardens were divine. If we had just known, we could've brought a picnic lunch, lain on a blanket on the pristine lawn, sipped some wine, and fed each other bread, olives, and cheese by the blooming flowers or under the trees. The tranquility of the property folded us under its wings.

A darling old couple told me Matisse was buried in the petite cemetiere on the other side of the monastery. As we mistakenly looked through the grand cemetiere, I thought I heard a baby cry. It could have been a cat or a bird—probably was. But we had to search to make sure there wasn't a frightened baby that someone had left, hoping a holy father or mother would find the child and bring him or her up. The crying stopped before we found the gravesites of Monsieur and Madame Matisse (and I had a slight neurotic worry that the baby wouldn't be found).

Matisse may have spurned her in life, but they have found eternal togetherness. Do death and life work like that? Is life death, and death life? Are they sometimes traded or confused? I laid flowers on the tombs for the artistic couple, as well as a flower for my mother, Bobbye Ann.

Driving back down the hill, we stopped at the Musée Marc Chagall. I count Chagall among my favorite painters, along with Matisse, and so was excited about seeing it. To paraphrase myself, wow. I'd read that the theme of these pieces was Biblical, and I've always been drawn to the mystical aspects of Chagall's work, but these were 17 canvasses that were huge, dynamic, poetical blasts of color and energy like the sound of heavenly music on the scale of Wagner's Ring (though not so authoritarian). Or they could be the life of dreams or the dreams of life, a journey into soulful creation that Chagall saw and felt. I hate to say this with my tremendous admiration for M. Matisse, but M. Chagall's museum blew M. Matisse's away.

What a brilliant day to find such emotion expressed in these visions with which two artists have endowed the world! These were spiritual. They were creation. This is what life is about.

When art and artists are seen as not being worthwhile, not worth being supported, not worth keeping on a school curriculum—especially in my own country—I have to ask what do we value? Material things (like at The Negresco) is the easy answer—money, power, winning over any and all competition. Is this fulfilling? Is this what soothes our souls and comforts us in the end? When "family values" are discussed among politicians, what does this really mean? Why aren't we teaching our children that true happiness comes from finding themselves, their own spirits, and expressing themselves in a meaningful way—and, in the process, contributing to the good of the world?

Their search for themselves is the search for God, and that is what will sustain them.

CHAPTER TWENTY-SIX
Lily of the Valley

WE WERE DRIVING through billowing clouds along the Corniche, and moment by moment the vapors surrounding us were pierced by stunning views of storybook villages floating on peaks and mountains plunging steep into turquoise sea. The scented air hummed with a profusion of herbs and flowers, while blossoms of hot red, magenta, yellow, purple, and pink burst in our vision. No wonder the glamour pusses who can afford to go anywhere in the world choose this.

Every village, town, or city that we saw or passed through had its allure. Eze and La Turbie were aeries in the sky for eagle people to fly in and land. Menton was a garden delight, with seaside café tables bearing hula-skirt umbrellas to shade the hot sun. Crossing the border into Italy was barely slowing down, but once we drove through the tunnel, the landscape was transformed. It was less developed and not as crowded as the French Riviera. Terraced hillsides covered with vineyards replaced a grid of multi-million-dollar houses.

I'd been wondering if there were any authentic fishing villages or seaside towns unspoiled by hordes of tourists left on the Mediterranean. Was this coast of Italy less crowded than France? From our initial impressions, it seemed so. The village called Latte looked nice, and quieter. It wasn't dripping with perfect re-do. We both had this feeling and noticed a lovely and large villa by the sea that could be brought back to life.

Jim says Italy doesn't call to him. Not to me either. I would be happy to spend a season in, say, Lucca or Sienna, for which we felt a pull. But France is my love. France feels like home to me, though I believe we could live in many places—not for good but for a few months here and there. In fact, this is how I want to live my life and have for many years. It's the way artists have always drawn fuel. We have short attention spans, a need for ever-changing stimulation, a need to experience our worlds besides in our heads. Our brains have to be restarted periodically with new sensory input, which then must be processed before spitting out our work. It can be done in other ways, but there's a reason that Matisse, Hemingway, and countless others like them chose the lifestyles they did.

Since we've been homeless, where and how we want to live is a continual discussion. I've loved our nomadic life. Constant change has been fulfilling—maybe because I was in one place so long. There are two ways we could go: 1) Travel with few belongings. 2) Keep a base somewhere and come and go. The first has proved impossible so far. Our car is stuffed. As writers, we have to have our equipment—computers, printer, files, books (and lots of them), etc. Plus, I've never learned the art of packing light. I'd bring my whole closet if I could. The second still leaves the questions of where the base should be, and what do we do with all our belongings in storage? To be honest, being homeless is still engaging to me. I'm not dying to have the responsibility of a house and all that that entails.

Spending time in Nice has made Italy more appealing. But suddenly we were driving along the Italian coast without a view of the sea. From one centro to the next, it was an endless line of cars like the urban sprawl of California. We finally arrived in San Remo, on which we'd set our sights for a nice lunch, but we couldn't figure out where, and we were starving. We were looking for dejeuner with the amusement of observing a restaurant scene with Eurotrash. It took forever, but we finally found one by the biggest yachts in the harbor. The restaurant wasn't actually on the water, but the gnocci and Caprese salad were so amazing they made up for it. Eurotrash sightings were gratified. There were two young couples of pudgy men and wafer thin women sporting cropped clothes and designer accessories, and a table of old stodgy women dressed in suits with one leftover husband to escort them. Then there was a group of men, women, and children and we could never figure out who went with whom.

Traffic was bumper to bumper on our return. It was a French holiday, and we were getting a taste of the summer nightmare. I hopped out in Menton to snap some photos while we inched through the street, but the angle was no good. As I headed toward Jim, the traffic speeded up. Before long I was running behind the car trying to catch up, or at least to get Jim's attention, but he was driving along daydreaming and didn't see me. The people behind us must've been laughing their butts off. I was laughing myself while I ran, before he finally slowed down long enough for me to dive in the car.

* * *

THE NEXT MORNING we packed up our Peugeot station wagon with our massive luggage, files, art books, and all the other stuff we'd added along the way. Le Grimaldi's chic owner, Joanna Zedde, had presented me with a gift. It was a Lily of the Valley planted in a purple cachepot with beautiful pink paper wrapped around it. She explained that it was a French tradition to give Lilies of the Valley for happiness on the May 1st holiday. I was touched by her thoughtfulness and named my dear lily, Lilianne. Along with Frida Kahlo, this made three girls to Jim's one male—just the way we like it. I found Lilianne's place in our Peugeot, and we said goodbye to fabulous Francoise and the other wonderful staff members. It is always sad to leave a place we've grown fond of, but we were excited as well. We were on our way to Corsica, where the Matisses spent their honeymoon.

When the ferry arrived, it was enormous. After parking our car onboard, we climbed the stairs to find our comfortable and roomy seats. The Mediterranean felt as smooth as silk as the ship glided over it. The mix of people ranged from families with babies to a group of senior citizens who were having lots of fun. One couple was dressed for another century. The man sported an old-fashioned suit from the early 1900's, with a straw boater plopped on his head, and he sauntered up and down the quay (and later ship) holding a wooden cane and pair of gloves. It was burning hot outside. Thank God the ship's cabins were crispy cool. I wanted to follow this couple around to see what they did and where they went, but didn't. Instead, I sat and watched the water slipping by me.

Water has played an important part in my life. My family loved to swim and play in it. My father died in it. One of my brother Brent's last happy dreams was of swimming with whales. The year before Jim and I left for France, we took Mother to a friend's charming lake cottage for Thanksgiving and, later, her birthday. Some of her happiest moments were being in or by the water. She enjoyed swimming and skiing or just watching it. It brought her peace, so she treasured spending these long weekends with us when we cooked and pampered her so she could be carefree.

As the huge ship cut through the blue Mediterranean, I thought of my mother and how much she would also have loved this, and I wished she were with us. I wanted her not to be dead, but I pictured her in a field of Lilies of the Valley with water lapping all around.

CHAPTER TWENTY-SEVEN

House of Dreams

AFTER LEAVING CORSICA, we arrived in luminous Nice and spent one night at the Hotel Beau Rivage, from whose windows Henri Matisse painted many of his earliest pictures of Nice and the Bay of Angels. Location, location, location. The Beau Rivage is a little tired for a four-star hotel, but you walk out the door and the life of the city surrounds you—the Promenade des Anglais around the block, the Cours Saleya down the street. We were happy to be back in Nice, where we felt we belonged. When you're homeless as we are, it's interesting to see what creates the feeling of home. One factor I can tell you is people. Even if you're in a hotel and the staff is warm, welcoming, personal, and helpful, they actually provide the comforts of home, the familiarity of a home, even the sentiment of an extended family—maybe nicer than your own!

In Nice, Le Grimaldi had been a home for us. Now we stopped by there to say good-bye and retrieve the rest of our belongings, which they had so kindly stored while we were in Corsica. With all the recent extras we had acquired, our car was more than stuffed with *stuff* for the short trip to Vence—and the huge Matisse payload which awaited us there.

We found the Matisse Chapel right away, and that was a thrill. We also knew that Villa La Reve, the house Matisse lived in for some six years during World War II, was right across the street somewhere. We ended up asking a nun to point it out to us. Villa La Reve—the House of Dreams: What could be a more mystical and mysterious name for the place where Matisse produced some of his most famous paintings— paintings Jim and I especially love.

We pulled into the driveway. The yard was wild and wonderful like "The Secret Garden" I loved so much as a child—natural and unruly, as though French hippies lived there in a "Grey Gardens" sort of splendor. The house itself—now owned by the city of Vence—had once been grand but was in a bit of disrepair. Yet it was plenty charming enough for me to see myself in it for a very long time.

We knocked on the door but no one was home. Joelle Audrey, who manages the house for the city fathers, had told us on the phone that she might be gone when we got there—she had to go pick up her daughter at school. We wandered around for a while, looking at this and that, peering in windows. Then a car pulled into the driveway. It was Joelle and her pretty daughter, Sourya, who has perfect café-au-lait skin, big brown eyes, and long hair flowing with waves. We liked them both immediately.

In season, Joelle books art tours at Villa Le Reve—artists and their groups of lucky students come and live for a while and paint here. Oh, Heaven for them—and for us. Joelle took us to the room where we would live for the next three days—it had once been Matisse's studio! This was the room in which he had created color and captured light and poured it all into his harmonious canvases. This was where he'd pinned his *Jazz* cut-outs to the wall.

The room was plain, though large, with a good-sized balcony looking out onto the famous palm trees that appear in so many of Matisse's paintings from this period. When M. Matisse was the resident, our room and the one next door were joined in a dramatic chamber of impressive size and quality. Unfortunately, the woman who'd owned the house before the city bought it had made the residence into a girl's school. She chopped up the big rooms and added showers and sinks with dormitory-style warrens of toilets. She lowered the high ceilings and covered them with ugly acoustical tile. This was a tragic rendering of the villa but didn't diminish our enthusiasm in the least. Jim was simply out of his mind. He was reeling with joy to be actually sleeping in the studio of his hero, and I was a gleeful follower.

We put our things away and then celebrated our good fortune with a lovely glass of wine on our balcony—Matisse's balcony. Then we drove into the center of Vence for a "gastronomique" dinner. It was the first time that we had seen a drink-and-wine package with such a meal, and it was worth the extra money. As we enjoyed our aperitifs of Champagne, I chatted up our fabulous waiter who was a stunning black man with stark white hair. Originally from Guadeloupe, he had come to Vence from Paris five years earlier to visit a friend, and he never left.

Had he found his own villa of dreams as we had found ours? Or was it a sunny life in Southern France with the spirits of Matisse and Chagall and the others who danced in Vence's air that captured him? Vence could make a good home, we thought, and we knew exactly where we wanted to live.

CHAPTER TWENTY-EIGHT

Days of Heaven

W
E ARRIVED AT Villa Le Reve planning to stay three days and ended up staying five. The truth is, we could've happily stayed another week or four. I had intense dreams in Matisse's room, but they weren't the creative ones I had wished for. There was too much turmoil coming from Arkansas about my mother's house and things, pressures that didn't need to exist at this particular time. In Matisse's villa of dreams, mine were nightmares—though it didn't alter my joy in being there. An exhilarating energy ran through the house. We felt like we were riding the top of a wave.

We were almost completely cut off from any media. There was no time to read *Le Figaro*, no telephone or TV, no Internet connection. Our first full day there we declared as a day of R & R, and we needed many more of them. Seeing new sights, hearing new sounds, being in a different milieu almost constantly is a huge amount of sensory information, knowledge, and change for a brain and body to process. Following M. Matisse's path, searching out the beauty and art that exists everywhere in France—it was exhilarating but draining. It was important for us to understand the villages and cities in order to grasp the big picture of Matisse's life and art, to see what he saw and imagine the ambience that inspired him. It was unadulterated happiness, but our brisk schedule was not.

After Matisse left his home region of Picardy, he either lived in Paris, Nice, or Vence or traveled to incredible settings to paint—and he would stay for three or four months wherever he went. He had the luxury of time to absorb and assimilate the colors and scenes, the towns and people before him. There was also the simple fact that Matisse was in his own culture, and we were learning a new one. In our journey, cost and a deadline were also factors. We tried not to stop anywhere for less than three nights, but that wasn't always possible. When we could stay longer, it allowed us to slow our pace. One of the best ways to gain awareness and insight is to make the effort more effortless—i.e., being somewhere for an extended time allows the environment to seep in unobtrusively and permits perception to grow.

Besides following Matisse, this was our journey too. We were changing our lives, seeing anew for ourselves. We needed time for reflection. Certain life events like Mother's death can't even be imagined, much less scheduled. We're not long-term planners anyway. We like our options open as long as possible, so we can change our minds, stay or go. No matter what—part of this passage had to be our own.

So this first day was one for Jim to paint on his hero's balcony, where the master himself looked out every day and created his visions. Jim wore his classic Panama hat while painting with passionate abandon. He had a grand time. I worked on my Diary, though I was having problems with my Dell computer. Little did I know they would plague me for months to come.

Matisse's Chapelle du Rosaire was open at two o'clock certain days for tours, and I had told Joelle Audrey that I wanted to go to church at *la chapelle*. She wasn't so sure about that, explaining that the nuns who run the chapel lock the doors once the service begins. "They lock you in and you can't leave until it's over," she said. I told her I didn't care.

On the day we went, we arrived five minutes late and the tour had already begun—in French, of course. But we turned and looked and nodded our heads following the nodding and oohs and ahs of everyone else, as if we understood the words as they did. The stained glass and tiles were vibrant and whimsical, but the chapel is small. Matisse viewed this installation as the culmination of his life's work. Imagine the weight of his will focused on this single idea.

But the longer I stood in this very tight space, the more I understood what Joelle had meant. I wanted to run—and I mean run *screaming* out of those locked wooden doors. Acute panic had struck, but I was afraid of the stern nuns who seemed ominously capable of punishment if you stepped out of line. So I stoically kept my mouth shut except for one slightly desperate whisper to Jim. I'm not saying anything depraved, such as the chapel isn't perfectly stunning. It is—as long as a claustrophobic torture chamber is what you're up for.

I have to admit that the first image that caught my attention was the Blessed Virgin with Her Child. But Matisse's Mary wasn't run-of-the-mill. Matisse's Mary was naked. That's right, she wore not a stitch. I couldn't recall seeing a single nude Virgin before, but this was the image Matisse chose to portray her in his most important piece of art. What did he see when he created her? What did he see when he gazed on her—the natural innocence of her state? Or the true importance of what counts in life as demonstrated by how one enters and leaves this world?

On another day we motored the short distance from Vence to St-Paul-De-Vence, the charming hilltop village that is home to the renowned restaurant La Colombe d'Or. Painters such as Matisse, Derain, Picasso, Dufy, Braque, and others traded their art for meals at this local eatery, and lunch at La Colombe d'Or and a view of those paintings were on our to-do list while we were so close by.

We walked through the garden doors of La Colombe d'Or, sans reservation, and I think it was quite remarkable that we got a table, considering the crowds. The jardin and view were glorious. Some American senator was lunching on our left and a Hollywoodish group held court on our right. The centerpiece of the latter group was an African-American actor-athlete-musician-businessman—we couldn't tell what he was, though he was wearing a beautiful woman as his most elegant accessory and talking on the phone a lot. He was dressed in a baggy basketball uniform and was soon joined by a man who spent a lot of energy sucking up to him.

When we didn't order a three-course meal, which was larger and more expensive than we wanted, there was a discussion between our waiter and possibly the manager. It seemed to be about whether they would let us stay with such a picayunish request for our repast. But they did, and we enjoyed a wonderful lunch of two entrees (first courses). The first was an assiette of crudités, which I have ordered several times before but not like this. They must have brought 20 little bowls and plates of everything from anchovies to eggplant to lentils to pates. It was a feast in itself for three or four adults, but we'd also ordered shrimp that were huge and good as well.

Afterwards, we wandered through the dining room, where we gazed upon some of the celebrated art, including a Matisse. Were they the originals? I don't know, but how could such treasures be left on the walls with such hordes of people coming and going? Anyway, we were glad we had seen it, because we didn't intend to pass this way again. In the afternoon we were off to another St-Paul institution, the Fondation Maeght. I was not bowled over by the Maeght collection either, or at least what I saw of it or the exhibition at the time. The Maeghts were obviously knowledgeable, sophisticated, and connected to some of the greatest artistic talent of the 20th century. They had an "eye." Does it make me a blockhead not to have taken much pleasure in these works, or at least the portion I saw of them?

One day we drove up into the hills to Grasse, and on another we visited Renoir's home in nearby Cagnes-sur-Mer. But wherever we traveled in that beautiful region, we were always happiest coming home to Villa Le Reve. Sometimes we would sip pastis outside with Joelle as Sourya played near the table. One night we took them out to dinner. Another afternoon Joelle introduced us to her neighbor, a man I will call M., who had lived in his charming 400-year-old house across from Villa La Reve for 50-plus years and had known Matisse personally. He told us priceless stories about Matisse and his long-term companion, Lydia.

Packing up on our last night there, we hated leaving Villa Le Reve. There is something inexplicably compelling about being in an artist's house and studio, where his daily life and work are filtered through his space and furnishings, the colors on the walls, the patterns in the textiles. In artists' studios, art and life are one. I felt safe in the big chopped-up house and wild garden, and Jim was lost in the spirit of Matisse.

But it was time to get on the road again.

CHAPTER TWENTY-NINE

A Little Piece of St. Tropez

COMING AND GOING, staying and leaving had defined our lives for many months. For me, the leaving always carried a bit of sadness—losing a new territory (in both France and in myself) that I'd only just found. Almost invariably, I wanted to experience more than the sites we *had* to see for the purpose at hand, but there weren't enough hours in the day to fully explore. I want it all. Whether beauty or culture, history or cuisine, something always intrigued me. I wanted to know the meaning behind the vistas. I researched and read, asked questions of anyone I could, and tried to "get" enough of the landscape and its people to feel that I knew them. But there was always much I still didn't know.

Leaving was also the most difficult for Jim, because he hated loading the car with the scads of baggage we were now carrying. It's not that I blamed him, but he grumbled and moaned until he was in a foul mood—and took his sweet time getting over it. Leaving Vence was especially hard. Matisse's house, Villa Le Reve, was a raw jewel. More than 50 years after Henri Matisse had lived there, it still held a piece of his creative force, and we hadn't even begun to mine all its secrets. As I've said previously, we could've happily stayed for months. Joelle, Villa Le Reve's manager, had been spectacularly kind and generous, essentially giving us the run of the place. We even had our own house key. Returning to the road meant tearing ourselves away from Matisse Mecca. Once again it felt like leaving home.

Yet along with our moping was sweet anticipation of the next adventure, and on the morning we drove away from Vence we were headed to Antibes. We got there to find the quaint market folding its tents, one robust man singing a French ballad as he packed the last of his inventory. Our lunch was a sandwich, and our dessert was a tour of the Picasso Musée with its stunning views of the sparkling blue sea. After visiting that museum, I admired Picasso more than I ever had before. This museum, and the body of work on display, is a wonderful tribute to Picasso's genius. He may've been mean, especially to women, but he seems to have been more generous with his endowments than Matisse was. Is leaving a tremendous legacy to your own museum a sign of more, or less, ego? Did Matisse sell his away and not have much left? Did he need the money?

From Antibes, we moved inland to Vallauris for a look at the town and its ceramic tradition—which Picasso revived by taking a shine to working with clay. Shops lined the main avenue, and since dishes are a particular penchant of mine, I practically had to slap my hand to keep from buying a wonderful brown, black, and turquoise plate with a classical picture of a woman in the center. It was the work of an artisan whose name I don't remember, but whose skill I certainly admired. If I returned today, I would buy it. And Picasso? A shop called Madoura has the rights to sell copies of his pieces—just so you know, in case you're burdened with a leaning such as mine.

As the Cannes Film Festival was in progress, we chose to skip Cannes. The irony of that amused me. For many years, my heart would've exploded to be able to attend it. It's not that I wouldn't still adore being in the thick of that scene, but—inexplicably—an invitation hadn't turned up. Just as well: Time was short, and there was much on our agenda. Besides, there was no Matisse connection to Cannes.

Not so with St. Tropez, where we headed next. Many people talk about the snootiness of this former fishing village, but almost all the plush hotels had wanted to welcome us with a discount (emphatically *not* the case anywhere else on our extensive itinerary). Matisse had spent the summer of 1904 here visiting painter Paul Signac, and despite the town's well-known glitz, art and artists are still a part of the St. Tropez culture.

We checked into the divine Hotel Le Yaca, and soon our bags were delivered to our luxurious room—which also opened onto the pool and garden. Le Yaca is a salve for the weary body and soul, and we immediately conked out on the elegantly appointed bed, napping a bit before heading down to the harbor to gawk at the massive yachts.

Talk about a scene: While imbibing a drink at the harborside Café de Paris, Jeem and Beth Joade, recently of the stuffed Peugeot station wagon, gaped at what might have been an episode of Robin Leach's "Lifestyles of the Rich and Famous." Yachts with staffs, staffs with uniforms. We thought some of Cannes' celebrity festival-goers might have cruised down the coast to St. Tropez, but no star-sightings awaited us.

The next morning, as we sat in the garden relishing our poolside coffee, my thoughts drifted back and forth between France and the U.S. In the wake of my mother's death and our return from her funeral, bitter words had been arriving from Arkansas almost daily in my email. This created waves of worry and stress that rolled through my grief. In addition, Mother's death had been the final blow in a year of changes that had overwhelmed our daughter Bret, and she had just—while we were in Nice—made a pivotal decision to drop out of school for the next year.

As I sat in that lovely Le Yaca garden, I knew our adventure had created fallout that we never could have foreseen but were now forced to cope with. I was trying to find my center and be true to these issues of being a good mother, losing my own, and forging ahead in this incredible journey that had been my, and our, dream. It was a constant rub. But in the complex workings of the human mind, distraction can be a useful tool. St. Tropez was full of them, and I threw myself into them in search of respite.

The high season, with all its reputed haughtiness, hadn't started yet, and so the village wasn't clogged with visitors, and "The Gold Chain Quotient," as Jim called it, was still blessedly low. We had time and space to enjoy the astonishing Musée de l'Annonciade. The paintings of Paul Signac anchored the collection that also included wonderful works by

Matisse, Vuillard, Bonnard, Braque, Dufy, Van Dongen, and others. The museum was small, manageable, and showed one of the best collections we'd seen anywhere in France.

One day, for eight euros each, we took a tourist boat ride around St. Tropez's bay, and it was worth every centime to be cruising the sapphire Mediterranean with the other sailboats and yachts. We glimpsed multi-million-dollar villas, the filming of a French soap opera, the less dramatic house of actress Bridgette Bardot, and a long black line of villagers in their funerary march down the hillside to the seaside cemetery.

Later that evening we happened upon a milling crowd, including men with fifes and drums. A local restaurant owner explained that this was the dress rehearsal for the next day's Bravades, the parade that commemorates the anniversary of the running aground of the boat carrying the decapitated head and body of the actual Saint Tropez. The Town Captain and his officers led the procession, and it was such a festive and joyous occasion that Jim and I marched along with the boisterous crowd. We circled the whole village, feeling part of the energy and spirit of this beautiful place.

For that brief moment, we were locals. Even though tomorrow we would have to pull up stakes again, a little piece of St. Tropez would be traveling with us.

CHAPTER THIRTY

The Last Supper

WE LEFT OUR luxurious little nest at Hotel Le Yaca as the *real* Bravades procession wove through St. Tropez. We could hear the fifes and drums while we loaded the car.

Jim and I were having our Leaving Spat that couples the world over engage in whenever they're trying to get out of town and go *anywhere*. This time it took the form of whether Jim should get in touch with a friend of a friend, who happened to live in the area. He didn't want to do it, which was true to form. He knows that if I think something is important, *I'll* do it. And in fact I did (and do) think that making contacts in a foreign country—expanding our circle—is something that's eminently worthwhile.

I admire this typically male behavior in some regards. It's pleasing, as well as efficient, to do only what *One* wants, what *One* is interested in, and what is of the import to merit *One's* attention. But usually for us females (inevitably me), this leads to being knee-deep in One's manure because it's in my/our best interest for whatever it is to get done. Another appropriate appellation for wives could be "Pack Mules." Hee-haw, hee-haw!

We wound through the hills and vineyards to make our way to Aix-en-Provence, which wasn't technically on our Matisse itinerary—but Henri Matisse greatly admired the painter Paul Cézanne, who hailed from Aix, and had bought one of his paintings when the Matisses could ill afford it. Matisse kept the picture for many years as a touchstone of sorts, a prized possession that he wouldn't part with, no matter what.

We'd been in Aix only one time before and had visited Cézanne's studio back then. I know I've written before about the joy of visiting an artist's studio, but how can I help myself? Visiting the room where great art has been made is a peep into the artist's vision of both art *and* life. I find that the creative energy lingers, and the choice of art, objects, and furnishings with which the artist surrounds himself forms a kind of parade (parades are still on my mind!) of the artist's dreams. Cézanne's studio was no exception.

The one day we were previously in Aix it was hot as Hades, as my mother used to say. I've learned from too many scorchers that even lovely locales such as Aix can lose their charms when I'm roasting. All I want to search for is a mother of an air-conditioner, which may well be in our car while it's speeding out of town. This time Aix was warm but *not* hot as hell, and we discovered a beautiful village shaded by luxurious plane trees and cooled by bubbling fountains suitable for water nymphs.

Our chosen hotel, the Grand Hôtel Négre Coste, was a handsome old shabby-chic inn on Aix's delicious main street, the Cours Mirabeau. The hotel was perfect for us, with a friendly, helpful staff. I had read that jazz musicians stay here when they're in town. It's that kind of place.

For me, another draw of Aix was the late writer M.F.K. Fisher. I love Fisher's work, her writings about food and her life in France. As a single mother living in Aix, she would pick up her daughters after school and take them to Les Deux Garçons for a treat of Chantilly while she indulged herself with a whisky. Now *that's* a woman to admire! I'd like to follow Fisher's trail around France—stay in her chosen hotels, dine in her restaurants, and prepare her special recipes. She once wrote about a hotel in Dijon that had wine on tap in all of the bathrooms. It can't possibly exist now (can it?), but I'd like to find out. Can you imagine how handy that would be? Of course Jim and I walked down the boulevard to Les Deux Garçons. It's not the same as during Fisher's time there, but I drank a whisky in her honor. To M.F.K. Fisher, salut!

I found a good stationery store in Aix, which pleased me since I hadn't been able to find one at all in St. Tropez. As much as I'd liked

St. Tropez, I found it sort of frightening that one could buy a rasher of bikinis but no pen cartridges or diaries. People can write while lying on the beach. The activities of sun worshipping, seeing-and-being-seen, and writing notes don't have to be mutually exclusive.

Our friend at the hotel, Ricardo, recommended Les Agapes for dinner. When we found it, tucked away on a tiny rue, we were pleased by its ambience, rusticity, and intimacy. A corner fireplace was used to grill the meat. What is it about watching your dinner being cooked that makes a person's mouth water? Are the aromas more intense? Is it the act itself, the cozy feeling that you're in the kitchen with the chef—or in someone's home? People love to gather in a kitchen. It's the center of action, the heart of the house where a family's love comes out in a meal to be shared. This was the feeling of Les Agapes. I savored a delicious brandade for a first course, lamb for the next, while Jim ordered salmon with avocado to begin and duck to end. It was a wonderful meal, and Aix-en-Provence was another place I'd like to return to—maybe next time in the cool Fall or Winter.

But this night marked the end of our time on the road chasing Matisse. The last supper, so to speak. The next day we would pack up our car for the final time—technically—in our journey. We would be heading to Collioure (yes, Gerard's perfect top-floor apartment did come through!) so Jim can finish writing the book in the spot where Matisse discovered the power of color. Tomorrow night, we would be in our new home away from home.

But while it was the end—or nearly so—of our following in the footsteps of Henri Matisse, it wasn't the end of the chase. The idea behind *Chasing Matisse* is living the life that calls you, and that's a journey that never ends.

What will be around the next corner for me—for us? I don't know, but I'm determined to see it through, to create the life I want. Freedom is a word we all love, but the most cherished freedom of all is to find our own truths—and, in that, to live life with the integrity to be ourselves.

CHAPTER THIRTY-ONE
Life in Collioure

WE SPENT 13 months in the village of Collioure on the Mediterranean Coast, with the Pyrenees Mountains rising behind us. I had always imagined us living in a fishing village, and that's just what Collioure had been until the town's livelihood changed from fishing to tourism. We were fortunate enough to find a small loft in a village house that was freshly renovated. Everything in it was spanking new except the thick wooden beams that sliced across the ceiling of our living room. As the ceiling dropped to the sides of the house, the beams were of head-banging height, and at times the top of Jim's head was bloody from all the knocks he'd gotten from forgetting to duck. He just didn't ever learn. Jim told our landlord that the flat should come equipped with a pair of motorcycle helmets.

French doors led to a petite balcony from which we had a spectacular view of voluptuous vineyards, a grand chateau, and an old fort. Not bad, as M. Malric of Paris' Hôtel St. Germain would say. While Jim wrote *Chasing Matisse*, I fought with Dell over my non-working computer, listened to French lessons on CD, read French history along with other books that had been stacked up for years, began exploring this richly rewarding countryside, and grieved the loss of my mother.

In late September, with the first draft of Jim's book done, we flew home to Arkansas to deal with my mother's belongings. The idea was we'd be away for six weeks, but they turned into 14 long, hard ones. There was much sad and lonely work to do in shutting down the house my parents built, where my brothers and I grew up, where, after my father died, my mother laid oak logs in the fireplace for 35 more years. She had long since made the house her own.

Those days are gone. On our last day there, I shut the door and walked away.

My old life was officially over, and France welcomed me back with her graceful open arms.

We returned on January 6, 2004, to the city we love, Paris, its gray winter skies forming a soft canopy over the City of Light. This time we brought along one more soul to add to our illustrious group of three (surely you haven't forgotten Frida)—I'm referring to our schnauzer, Snapp, finally in France! Getting Snapp's papers had been troublesome, and our vet's office in Little Rock helped tremendously. Before we left the States, there was still one possible hang-up: If the weather was too cold, Snapp wouldn't be allowed to fly. January 5 dawned unseasonably warm in the U.S., but the Paris prediction was one degree too cool. The Delta agent was accommodating, willing to bend the rule if our vet faxed a letter giving her permission. The vet did, and they let Snapp onboard. At age 12 he flew from Roanoke to Atlanta to Paris—his first plane trips ever—and he did fine.

As I write this, he's been in his new country of residence for three weeks. The sights and smells have thrilled him, and he can't believe his good fortune in being able to go into stores and restaurants. His first experience in Paris was at the swanky department store called Le Bon Marche. Like an American gentleman, he rode the escalator up and perused the sales. It goes to show the old cliche is wrong. Old dogs *can* learn new tricks.

As always, the beauty of Paris filled my senses. How can you compare a radiant summer day to a silky winter evening with a walk along the Seine? Being in this city again was enthralling, but I also have to admit, it didn't seem as exotic. It felt familiar, even *natural,* to fly into Paris. Does that make it home? Is this the question we'll ask from now on? We still have roots in Arkansas, but our home is not there anymore. That life has been buried in the soil.

We found out after we'd returned to France how much Bret wishes we weren't so far away. Oh, we knew—but she had never expressed it so succinctly or directly. Did we leave too soon? Should we have waited another year or two, when she might've been more settled and confident in her own shoes? Does that time ever come?

As it was January in Paris, I had to hit a few sales. From our ever wonderful Hotel St. Germain at 88, rue du Bac, it was a skip down the vintage blocks with lovely stores to Le Bon Marche. I purchased a few items along the way, and they were then wrapped impeccably and beautifully as gifts for friends in France (as well as back in the States). On our last morning in this city—before we headed back to our apartment in Collioure, in the far Southwest—I broke down and made the irrational decision to buy my first real French lingerie. This humiliating experience may not be quite as bad as trying on swimsuits, but this is hard to gauge.

Le Bon Marche's lingerie department (which is too-too, frou-frou, and woo-woo) was packed full of women of all sizes and shapes. French women adore sexy bras, panties, bustiers, thongs, anything. They all wear them, and I suppose they all try them on. This supports my previous theory that French females accept their bodies (by their apparel or lack of it and conduct at the beach) publicly. They must go into those dressing rooms, see their own images, and like them fine or well enough to purchase these undergarments that are often scant and always have a come-and-get-me attitude. They are not going to buy boring or ugly. I went. I laid out my credit card. I got away from there. Man, oh man. (I guess that's the point.)

After a quick trip to Brittany and a lovely visit with Alice in Auray, we had a most pleasant drive through France. By the time we skirted around Toulouse, we had that "almost home" feeling. It was dark and rainy when we arrived in Collioure. We unloaded our packed-to-the-gills car and took Snapp up the elevator to his new abode. It felt a little strange because we'd been away so long, but we were happy to be here. We invited our friend Gerard up for a drink when he returned from dinner. We were glad to see his tall, angular self and to hear his voice.

The next morning we carried our straw bag to the Sunday market, where we bought roasted chicken and fresh vegetables. On this first outing, we ran into two more friends. One we met for coffee at Les Templiers. The other surprised us on the stone path that curves around the chateau with its demilune of sea. She'd also been away and had just returned the day before, as had we. She and her husband are Dubliners.

Since then, we have stocked the pantry and rearranged the furniture. We've even bought some new stuff—a funky 50's lamp and a 30's leather club chair. We've taken a few spectacular jaunts to see Pyrenees vistas we hadn't seen before, and we finally found a new bed for Snapp, who is settling in. Jim is working on revisions.

Collioure and our apartment are our own again.

CHAPTER THIRTY-TWO

My Circling Theory

IT WAS DIFFERENT now. The crowds were gone. The village was quiet. Most stores and restaurants were shut for rest and renovation. This had been happening before we left in September, but while we were gone Collioure had returned to herself. The feminine usage: She seems like a woman to me with her safe, liquid harbor and brightly painted skirt that surrounds it. Her home is wallpapered with vineyards and the Matisse blue of the sky, and her light is in the sunbeams. Like a siren, she calls artists, sailors, and searchers to come to her shores.

Though we'd missed a chunk of it, winter is the window of opportunity to really become part of the life here. The cold months are the time when residents warm to invaders such as we are. After the hordes have deserted, opportunities to have little chit-chats avail themselves and the Collioure natives open up—especially when you have a dog.

With Snapp along, more people spoke to us—which was mostly for the good. They stopped to pet him or compliment his well-groomed visage. But then there was the white-haired woman with her little white fluff dog who fussed at Jim about Snapp, because he was not on a leash all the time. It's possible that she was concerned about Snapp's safety and not Jim's canine etiquette—plenty of dogs run loose with their masters—but Jim didn't know. He didn't understand what she was saying, but he knew she wasn't happy with him. I keep telling one of my friends to get a dog, and she'll meet people. You know who you are. Get a dog, and you'll meet someone!

They say pets resemble their owners, and Snapp is the spitting image of Jim. His hair is peppered black, silver, and gray, and he sports a smart beard. Elegant and proud, he carries himself lightly, virtually prancing when he's feeling on top of the world. He loves to sleep, pouts when he doesn't get his way, and growls when he feels under attack for reasons imagined or real. Actually, Snapp looks more like Jim than either of his human sons do.

Collioure is French Commando headquarters, and winter is wonderful Commando watching time. Imagine a platoon of hunky muscles-bulging-through-their-camouflage French soldiers training to carry out war and survive. The other day one company was practicing getting their buddies across the canal in a rubber raft one by one. The rafter had to lie down with all his gear and guns, while on the beach another faction furiously pumped up other rafts. The idea seemed to be Commando vessels for a getaway to sea. There must be a requirement for the men to be good looking. Trust me on this, ladies. It might be worth a trip over. The "Sex and The City" nymphs would be hitching a ride for a hopefully happy ending—a Mediterranean sunset or at least a bumpy spree.

In Collioure when I was the morning walker of Snapp, we often followed the street that ran by the side of our house and which our balcony looked down upon. It was the last rue on this side of town, and though I hate to admit this, I wasn't able to identify which direction it was in the earth's magnetic field. I think I have known since I've lived here, but my memory fails me, and a natural sense of directional bearing is not one of the talents I happen to have. I think I used to be better at finding true North, and I've spent days and days in the car being our navigator and done very well—but then there are those moments in a city when I can't for the life of me look at a map and figure out how to get to where I want to go.

This is made worse because France is a country that spins you round and round in circles wherever you are, and I mean that quite literally—so when you come out the other side of a rond-point you're never quite sure which direction you're headed. This must be just as much the case for those who aren't impaired at finding their bearings. There are loops on narrow rues and big highways and at turning points to go anywhere. I don't know how long the physical road structure has been this way. Did 12th-century pilgrims on their way to Santiago de Compestela hike around these spherical intersections looking for a sign to point their way to the bones of St. James?

The good thing about the roundabouts is that you can have as many chances as you want to determine your route, instead of making a wrong choice and driving seemingly forever down a road looking for a place to turn around. Jim grumbles when he doesn't know where he is or which direction to go. I have learned not to be as nervous as I once was, because the other great advantage of the endless rings around everything in France, as well as the signage—whether a pig-trail of a small village rue or a four-lane city boulevard—is that sooner or later there are always signs to Toutes (all) Directions that one can follow to find his way anywhere.

It has recently come to me that this institution of dizzying circles is a symbol for more than the traffic routes in France. On television, talking heads are forever discussing whatever-it-is, which doesn't stop for more salacious prime-time trash, bad sit-coms, or the culmination of some stupid reality show to elevate ratings. And if you've read Polly Platt's book, *French or Foe*, you understand that nothing gets accomplished in French business meetings except talking and talking and more meetings to come. I also learned from her that engineering is one of the most prestigious professions, and my circling theory comes to a gyrating point with them and the architects. I've lived here long enough to appreciate some innovations and to recognize that others (like some modern architecture) are original but bad. I think the competition to produce something inventive must be quite intense.

With my circling theory, I recognize that looping round and round in life is culturally apropos here. Getting anywhere as the crow flies is not the French way.

When Snapp and I amble up the rue, a high stone wall shelters us from the chilly wind. We pass by a tree loaded with lemons and a garden that an old woman lovingly tends. When we reach the end before the street curves toward the village, a tidy family house comes into our view. It is two stories with blue shutters, and even when the mornings are refreshingly cold, the windows are thrown open to a hillside of vineyards climbing to the sky.

I hear a rooster crow, and Snapp and I make the arc that takes us into town—and to the rue de Soleil that circles us back home.

CHAPTER THIRTY-THREE
Riders of The Storm

THE WIND HOWLED, and rain steadily pounded the roofs and streets, land and sea throughout the night. The leak in our skylight, that streamed down a framed poster of Matisse's "Odalisque á la culotte grise" for the first time when we were away, was back and silent drops of water were glazing the floor. I stayed up and read.

I was close to finishing Marie Antoinette by Antonia Fraser, and since I've become quite fascinated with "that Austrian woman," as the French would say as a slur during the lifetime of this much and wrongly maligned Queen of France (in Ms. Frazier's opinion and now mine as well), I couldn't put the heavy tome down.

I'd been on a course of reading French history to understand the roots of the country I'm in. I had gone from Middle Ages to Revolution, or, to put it another way, from murder, mayhem, and pillaging to murder, mayhem, and pillaging.

Some things don't seem to change in time—with the exception of who's doing it to whom. Constant warfare together with inhumane atrocities weren't a daily routine in the France of the 18th century, as they had been in the 11th and 12th, when survival often depended upon the whims of one's ruler and/or conqueror, as well as on the Pope and Church, and on what terror was improvised and who owed what revenge to whom. That is, until the people rose up against the royal family and aristocracy and chopped off so many heads that streets ran thick with blood. As the heads, hearts, and various other entrails of whoever was the last to be tried and found guilty of some treason real or made up were paraded upon pikes around town, the rioters were literally covered in the sticky red fluid that courses through life or drains from the lack of it. The radicals were evidently delighted to mutilate bodies, which is a bit disappointing, but the blood of their victims reflected some sort of (twisted and anti) communion with their freedom. The point of changing the system in France was valid; these actions were dubious at best. But this is inevitably the question of revolution: Must it be murderous and violent?

One day this storm would pass though martyred Queen Marie Antoinette, who desperately tried to protect her children and husband but in the end could not. Her nightmare of a tempest didn't stop until death found her on the guillotine, and she met it with grace and dignity.

I love a good storm and the uneven lament of the wind. My sun and moon chimes on the balcony were jangling so hard I worried they would be ripped apart and tossed to Ceret, but I left them alone. Even after I crawled under the covers at 2 A.M., I listened as the driving rain hit the tiles on the roof and the wind yowled through the black night.

Last Saturday in Collioure, the day after the storm, it rained on and off and the sea was in turmoil. Waves crashed and sprayed against the ramparts of the Chateau Royale and covered the path around it. There was no beach. Debris had washed up and down streets. Fervent surfers dressed in wetsuits caught and rode gigantic waves into a rock wall for shore.

In my dictionary of symbolism, the storm is said to represent "a powerful manifestation of the gods and their will." For me, it is true that part of a storm's attraction is its natural majesty, and in my novel *Innocent Lanier* the whole book is turned on a potent tornado that spins the characters' worlds around. I dream of these whirling winds as well.

If storms carry messages of the gods' will, then the world must have thundered when France revolted and massacred the establishment that needed to be reborn. And in a quieter fashion, a tempest blew again to split open the bindings of art when Matisse and Picasso covered canvas with their rich imaginings. They were riders of the storm that they themselves created, and they were lucky enough to catch the cultural wave and tame it.

But no matter where the lightning strikes, as the winds of change howl, so does man. We all must ride the storms that are thrown us. Or get bucked off and drown.

CHAPTER THIRTY-FOUR

Called By Color

THE IMMENSE MOUNTAIN that juts out of the Pyrenées-Orientals, Le Canigou, was magnificently robed in ermine snow with billowing white and gray clouds hovering over her. Canigou is usually our first sign of home, but this time she was our portent of leaving. We were racing up the highway to Toulouse, on our first big trip since returning to France—our first voyage for which we'd had to leave our good dog Snapp, who was being attended by our new American friend, Rachel.

We were pursuing another important passage in the chasing of Henri Matisse—I'm speaking of Morocco, where the scenes, colors, light, architecture, dress, and physical mannerisms of the people captivated his imagination and resulted in an important series of paintings. Our first stop from Toulouse was Amsterdam, and if you look at a map this makes no sense at all—but KLM offered cheap tickets, so we were flying to Morocco through the Netherlands.

We arrived in Casablanca at 11 P.M. It had been a long day, and we were happy to be met by our driver, Mr. Aziz Abou Ouafa, who would also become our caretaker, organizer, guide, and friend over the course of the next week. He delivered us to Le Royal D'Anfa Hotel (now Palace D'Anfa, but we were so excited that it was 2 A.M. before we laid down our heads.

Morocco had always been part of our plan in chasing Matisse. There was no question that this North African country inspired Matisse's vision and art. But when the Iraq war erupted in the spring of 2003, we backed off. Right or wrong, we were afraid it wasn't a good time for Americans to go. After returning to France in January 2004, we changed our minds, and I emailed Mr. Bennachir Akli at Olive Branch Tours, the company that had provided terrific escorted excursions when I'd made my first trip to Morocco five years before. I knew their expert services and wanted the guidance of Olive Branch this time as well.

The morning after our arrival, Aziz gave us a full tour of our teal Mercedes van that was loaded with amenities: DVD player, fold-out table, refrigerator, and roomy, comfortable seats—a luxurious ride for two travelers who had rocketed through France on their own steam. This was Jim's first sojourn to Morocco, and he didn't have to drive! For once, he could observe, take notes, and savor just being there. He could experience and process in real time without being burdened by logistical responsibility.

We glided through Casablanca on the Mercedes cloud while Aziz pointed out the attractions of his hometown. First stop was a tour of the enormous Hassan II Mosque, which is situated right by the Atlantic Ocean. The glorious mosaics of blues, greens, ochres, and golds gleamed in the sunny sky with the sapphire ocean lapping below. This is one of few Mosques that non-Muslims can visit, and it's more beautiful than I remembered. The colors were already calling Jim, and he had the space to really "see."

After that, we headed to Rabat. It was a smooth, beautiful ride with the blue Atlantic always in sight, and seaside villages popping up between long stretches of wild coastline. Whenever we were far from a city or town, we would see groups of two or three people just sitting beneath trees. We also noticed people hunkered down on almost any green space available—in the middle of what looked like pastures or empty urban lots. Jim said Matisse had painted people doing just that— but what *was* that they were doing? I asked Aziz if these areas were like parks, and he answered in the affirmative.

We were trying to understand this seemingly strange phenomenon, but it was several days before my "pasture sitting" theory took shape.

Historically, there must have been little need for parks. Men lived their lives outside, but women were concealed behind the plain exterior walls of their houses to live, work, and raise their children. A public social life was an oxymoron for the female gender. Their entire world was literally the interior, and most gardens occupied this space. Color, beauty, arts and craftsmanship in tiles, mosaics, fabrics, rugs, carved woods, plaster, even the garden plantings—all of it was only to be enjoyed by those invited inside. I've since read that the contrast between plain exterior and rich interior of the traditional houses indicated the sharp distinction between public and private life in Islamic society. Also, courtyards provided light, air, ventilation, and a place for protected activities in the hot and dusty climate. In other words, my theory wasn't half-bad. But with the difference between then and now, there is a niche for public green (or desert-flowered) spaces and urban landscape plans.

After a good lunch of lamb tajine and chicken couscous, we met our guide in Rabat, Mr. Ahmed Saadi, who speaks many languages fluently, is well educated and well spoken, and is insightful about his country's history and culture. He showed us the royal palace, the Tour Hassan, and the rapturous energy of an unfinished mosque. When it was begun by the sultan Yacoub al-Mansour in 1195, it was meant to be the largest mosque in the western Muslim world; but when the sultan died four years later, the work stopped. The unfinished shell remained a structural ghost until 1755, when an earthquake took down most of it. The tower, a chunk of wall, and the silent columns are all that remain. They spoke to us with what I believe was mythic power. Is this a typical tourist reaction? I have no idea.

Our final stop was the Kasbah. Who doesn't want to be taken to the Kasbah? Yet this voluptuous word is a trick, a wolf in sheep's clothing. Kasbah's definition is a fort or citadel, so I have corrected this unjust wrong and devised my own meaning. To correct your old dictionaries: Kasbah is a dreamland with cool ocean breezes, lush gardens, sumptuous palaces, and huge lounging chairs covered in filmy canopies. While mesmerizing music floats through the scented air, the healing gurgle of water runs through marble fountains. It is mandatory to relax in silken robes as comfy as pjs, lie on your chaise lounge, and read a good book while sipping mint tea.

Our actual stroll through the Kasbah was a breath of fresh air. We followed the path through a sensual garden, perused the shelves of a boutique selling books and art (a literary salon on some evenings), and relished the streets of houses painted blue and white for the union of sea and sky, their separate elements being fused in watery air. The doors made me happy. Most were painted some hue of blue but were also patterned with flowers and geometric shapes in purples, pinks, reds, oranges and other tones of sea and land. Many were decorated with the open palm of Fatima with fingers pointed up, which is a symbol to keep the powerful evil eye away. Who couldn't use one?

I think Ahmed might've been a little put out with silly us. I'm sure there were other objects or places of import to which we should've been paying more attention, but it was the vibrant Moroccan colors that had called our names so many years before, just as they had called Matisse. One Christmas, long before this project had entered our heads, Jim and I surprised each other with books about Morocco. Perhaps a wise purple and fiery red had foreseen our journey and were cabling us a preview?

CHAPTER THIRTY-FIVE
Woven Voices

I OPENED THE sliding glass door of our swish room in the Palais Jamais, which once was the palatial home of a grand vizier to the sultan. This posh hotel, an oasis in the Moroccan landscape, is one of my favorite places to stay in the world. As I stepped onto the terrace, the sun was up and shining, the air cool. I looked down upon the hotel's manicured Andalusian gardens and sapphire pool and, beyond, to the ancient medina that sprawled across the panorama. Its warren of path-sized streets and buildings bloomed with the minarets of scads of mosques. We knew they were there but not in such numbers.

The morning call of prayers had been our crowing rooster that someone was up, while dawn still had the good sense to hold back. I slid back into bed while Jim showered. Within minutes, a flock of petite birds were hopping into our room, flitting up on chairs and the foot of my bed. No doubt they had breakfasted on the plates of nuts, fruit, cookies, and crumbs of croissants in the elegant Palais many times before, but no luck with us. Our stash was covered, though the brave little birds added to my curious morning sensation that some people unwittingly refer to as cheerfulness; or in this case, perhaps it was the dizzy delight of waking as a sultaness.

Aziz was waiting when we made it out the door. He'd brought our first-rate guide for the next few days, Mr. Omar. Official guides in Fes wear djellabas, which are long flowing robes with attractive hoods that drape down the back or are pulled over the head. Men and women alike slip them over their clothes. They are the Moroccan national costume, and one sees them everywhere. I'm guessing George Lucas must have been introduced to Morocco before envisioning *Star Wars*, because his characters are fitted out in shades of this gear. The guides top themselves off with a maroon fez. Omar looked quite distinguished in his.

We took a short drive with a couple of stops along the way, but next was the medina, which I was dying for Jim to experience. I had taken this tour of Fes years before, and I knew how shocking this old center is to the Western sensibility. Picture a noisy human ant colony bustling through the business of the day. Enigmatic energy pervades the exotic sights, sounds, and smells that jolt the brain. Dyers of textiles, cutters and molders of brass trays and pots, weavers and woodworkers diligently work in dimly lit cave-like rooms with dirt floors to create the exquisite crafts for which Fes is known. Old wrinkled men with white beards and young men with black hair work briskly, and the traditions and skills are passed down to each new generation. The tanneries are outdoors with big vats of rank-smelling dye. One's eyes are agape, senses standing on end—when suddenly you're warned to jump out of the way for a donkey packing some sort of goods, even the garbage. No cars can get through.

The stalls of the sellers are jam-packed with fruits and nuts, djellabas and the cloth to make them, household essentials, spices, henna for hair dye and impermanent tattoos, brass works, and rugs. Fried fish, boiled eggs, breads, sweets, and brochettes are cooked and sold. Crates of live chickens are awaiting the ax or to be taken home by a buyer. The streets are alive with workers and shoppers, babies slung on their mother's backs. Darlings, it is madly untamed though not in the fashion of the old American West. It is rather a sense that time has stood still (though the life within continues at a furious pace).

The walls in the medina are centuries old and gloomy, so you can literally walk by a palace and never know. It's always the interiors that reveal the fantastic colors, fabrics, mosaics, and tiles of this culture. We stopped at several mosque doorways to get a glimpse of the rich inner sanctums, but tourists are allowed into the Medersa Bou Inania, a deep-rooted theological college and a striking example of the fine Moroccan plasterwork and woodcarving.

One of the most beautiful palaces you can visit in Fes is the home of the rug cooperative Aux Merveilles du Tapis, which has a huge selection of old and new Arabic and Berber carpets. I must alert you: It is dangerous to be surrounded by such beauty. One sits on a lush banquette and is served a glass of steaming mint tea while a selection of handsome carpets is brought for her scrutiny. The clever merchants start with the new ones, which, let me tell you, are something to shake a stick at. Then they tantalize you with the old ones, which have an opulent patina of age and design, a history of life that sings.

The last time I was in Morocco, one of my excellent guides from Olive Branch Travel told me the story of the women and their rugs. In the olden days, women were said to leave their house only twice—when they married and when they died. They might go to the hammam for a bath in the cover of night, but the point was that women weren't seen publicly—not in the mosques or even when male visitors came to their homes. The ladies were hidden behind screens through which they could peer. Their only close contact with a larger world was with female relatives, and they used their spare time to weave rugs in which they told their stories in symbols. Creating them was their outlet, their means of self-expression in which they could connect with themselves and the universal spirits who cosmically saw and heard them. How powerful! Madame Loves-All-That (me) felt conjoined in their sisterhood, their language in art and woven voices. I didn't buy a carpet back then, but we needed one now, and I had an idea this was my great opportunity. In other words, I set myself up. (I blame this penchant for acquiring beautiful things on my beloved mother and brother.)

Jim and I were drawn to the Berber pieces, which were patterned with tribal symbols and icons. Of course they were old ones. Jim stayed out of it, but after three hours of my-mama-was-Scotch/Irish haggling, we became the owners of les tapis de Maroc and at a miraculous third of the price from where we started. I like to bargain, but had never been at it like this—with pros. It was astonishing. Right place/right time/out of my mind, proud and pleased with myself. Jim tartly suggested the guilt would arrive later.

We consumed a delicious lunch starting with the typical first course of salads—various mixtures of aubergines, onions, courgettes, peppers, tomatoes, beets, carrots, olives, and beans slathered and cooked in olive oil and savory spices that define the distinctive Moroccan palette. Omar led us back through the snaking streets, and we made one last stop at one of the hand-painted ceramic shops. The plates, bowls, dishes, and mosaic tables of all sizes and shapes are another of the remarkable crafts found in Fes. I know which dinner-party-sized slab I want when I get my mas in the South of France.

What a brilliant, long, and exhausting day! But after freshening up, we continued on to dinner and maybe the best meal of our trip. La Maison Bleue is another old palace with a wonderful restaurant and rooms to be let where you can imagine Humphrey Bogart delivering his lines (this is one of my gauges for authentic and cool). Course after course of delectable food was marvelously delivered while mysterious North African music—the playing of lutes and the wailing of chant/songs—sounded through the room. The musicians danced while spinning the tassles on their fezzes.

* * *

AS I WENT to sleep, it was the voices of women—their chorus in carpets—that sang in my head.

(HAPTER THIRTY-SIX

On The Road

A S AZIZ DROVE us out into the Moroccan countryside, we saw many sheep with their herders; newborn lambs; donkeys carrying riders or gigantic water bottles, packages, God knows what. We stopped for cows to cross the road. Sometimes their front legs were tied together so they wouldn't wander too far away. I felt sorry for the hobbled animals. There were no fences anywhere.

The land was covered in verdant green grass that looked woven like the carpets, with neon orange flowers as their embellishment. Omar said that in two weeks time red poppies and blooms of blue and white would add to the vibrant landscape. Vineyards spread over plains, and men and women hoed the vines with their own steam. The plethora of satellite dishes that topped every house and building—no matter how primitive—seemed out of place.

We stopped in Meknes to see the stables of Moulay Ismail, the second sultan of the Alaouite dynasty that rules Morocco today. The stables once housed 12,000 fine Arabian horses that were cared for by 6,000 men. The Sultan had planned to build his own Versailles like his contemporary Louis XIV of France, though it was never finished. But the horses got their chateau, which was vast and impressive. Eighteen thousand people lived inside these cool, thick walls. Water was drawn by wooden wheels with leather pockets to refresh the thirsty steeds.

Moulay Ismail was supposed to have rocked the country with his cruelty. Clearly a man of great appetites, he had hundreds of wives and fathered a reported 800 children, the descendants of which now guard his tomb. He may have provided for the originals, but there must be too many to count in these later generations. We've heard that another man of celebrated appetites, Mick Jagger, has a house in Meknes. I prefer his brand of rock.

As we left the city, we saw a man tilling a hillside with a mule pulling an old-fashioned plow, a sign of the kind of agrarian economy that no longer exists in our own country. The rolling hills were covered in groves of olive trees. In some groves, great sheets were spread on the ground beneath the trees while men hit the branches with sticks to shake off their crop, and then bagged them up. As this work went on, women and children relaxed on pallets underneath the olive's shade. Two men sat and poured tea while their little lambs slept.

The countryside spread out before us like patchwork—rich dirt, lush fields, silvery olive trees. Omar says that if you cut an olive branch and give it plenty of water, it will grow. It is called the "tree of light," because the oil was burned in lamps. The Moroccan olives are rich and ripe, some of the best we've had anywhere. Somehow I didn't expect this fertile terrain here.

The temperature was hot (imagine the summer) when we arrived in Volubilis, yet another colony of the Roman Empire. I will say again, those Romans! Of course I studied them in history class, like everyone else—but that was for school, when I was more interested in getting a good grade than truly understanding what their record meant. But as I've traveled more and more, and I've seen their settlements throughout the world, I've gotten a sense of the vast Roman Empire which almost seems unbelievable in its scope and ambition—much less the administrative difficulty of keeping these strung-out colonies in line. No wonder there was constant war.

Volubilis is a stunning city built in the 2nd and 3rd centuries. The outlines of the houses and shops remain, along with the triumphal arch, baths, basilica, brothel, and capital—monuments of a bygone culture. But the mosaics are the thing—exquisite, detailed images and ancient design that's timeless in its beauty. Venus, Hercules, and Orpheus all had an address here. Those Romans knew how to live and to make things lovely, how to pick a position that held nature in its finest view—as do the current residents, who happen to be storks. No doubt these statuesque birds have good taste, since they've made their own massive nests on ancient columns and can command the scene around them.

It was another good but long day, and in the evening Jim and I decided to treat ourselves by ordering room service in the Palais Jamais for dinner. We needed our rest. Tomorrow we would head to major Matisse territory.

* * *

ALL ALONG THE road to Tangier, I noticed women picking some green leafy plant. Omar said it was called bakoua, and it makes a good salad. They carried it in bundles on their backs, like their babies. We were deep in the countryside, and I think for the first time I saw women riding donkeys. None was dressed in Western clothes. They all wore a piece of cloth—usually red and white striped—but sometimes stripes of yellow, green, and blue over some kind of pants. Matisse painted people in outfits like these.

We stopped in the Rif Mountains, at a village called Chaouen, for a lunch of salad and brochettes. Chaouen is a laid-back town, and Jim and I both liked it. We wandered around the medina with no crowds or dark streets. Sunshine poured into them. I wanted to find some of these Rif skirts and did, through a young Moroccan man who spoke great English and is engaged to an American woman from Chicago. His brother is already married to an American in the diplomatic corps, and they'll soon be going to the States to get ready for a transfer. These guys were cool, and Chaouen was a nice contrast to the big cities with their frenetic pace. It was quiet and easily manageable, the Rif Mountains majestic. Not a typical tourist destination with required agenda, which made it a relief.

But Tangier was where Matisse found his greatest inspiration, and so we left the peaceful countryside for the teeming port city—home of smugglers and pirates, robbers and spies, adventurers and artists, and even a few diplomats. Omar would leave us here—he had to return to Fes for a wedding. And we insisted, against Aziz's protestations, that he too leave us alone here for the next few days. It had been fun having guides, but now we wanted to explore the mystery of Matisse's Tangier at our own pace, day and night, on our own.

CHAPTER THIRTY-SEVEN
The Port of Tangier

OUR FIRST IMPRESSION of Tangier was of a big city with a big-city feel, though that changed. We checked into another incredible hotel, the El Minzah, an elegant jewel with a touch of shabby chic. Our room had a terrace with a spectacular view to the sea. The downstairs piano bar, with its cozy banquettes, was a wartime favorite of Allied bigwigs and various spies, and is said to have been the inspiration for Rick's "Café Americain" in *Casablanca*. Whether that's true or not, I could definitely see Humphrey Bogart holding forth there. The El Minzah so utterly evoked romantic visions of what a colonial hotel should be that we hardly wanted to leave it.

The Port of Tangier conjures up images of mystery and intrigue, of spies having secret signals and hushed conversations, of men slinking through the night like worn but agile tomcats, and of old gay men coming from the West to find solace and pleasure in their select young parallels. It is a city of and for men. I felt this nowhere else in Morocco, but these cafés told the tale. They are full of men huddled together in conversation, sipping their hot and sugary mint-infused tea, dragging on smokes, staring into the streets, their lives, their worlds. What do they see? So many of these men need work.

Unlike in France, women are almost completely nonexistent in Tangier café life. The only female we saw in one was a random European who must have been either very brave or very foolish. I'm a fearless traveler, but either I didn't have the courage or I had the good sense to skip this experience. I didn't feel unsafe, but the scene was a little creepy and didn't suit me. (If you want to debate the point that the whole of Morocco has this culture, I will agree theoretically, but Tangier is vastly different. It doesn't slide neatly into a Moroccan pigeon hole.)

We had been told that most tourists don't go to Tangier—that the life and cultural ambience of the city don't justify the time spent here. But this was the Moroccan city where Monsieur and Madame Matisse had lighted, and one of Henri's most famous series of paintings emanated from this period. Tangier was our ultimate Moroccan goal. I liked Tangier, then didn't, but swung back around with one important caveat. Tangier isn't easy. It is murky, intense, hard to read, and takes some time to navigate—inwardly, at least. For us, the effort was satisfying. I was glad we went.

To understand Tangier, you have to know a little of its history. The Greeks and then the Romans (with their Celtic cavalry) settled here before the Arabs arrived to war with the indigenous Berber tribes. Many other invaders took their turns as well. Tangier reminds me of Havana in that its location on the sea made it a prime target for all the aspiring nations who wanted to control its well-situated port.

Most of Morocco became a French Protectorate in 1912, and in 1923 the resolution among the competitors for Tangier was to make it an "international zone" that was run by diplomatic agents of Britain, Spain, France, Portugal, Holland, Italy, Belgium, Sweden, and the U.S. Tangier was wide open for bankers, libertines, exiles, refugees, artists, writers, and others for whom the "anything goes" posture of licit and illicit dealings packed a punch. Spy stories abound, and if Graham Greene didn't set a story in Tangier, he should have. The fun ended in 1956 shortly after the French handed Morocco back to its people and rulers, but there is still a leftover atmosphere of shady maneuvering.

The other important point in understanding Tangier, a short ferry ride from Spain, is that it's the entrance for Europeans coming into Africa—and also the gateway for Africans who are headed to Europe. A number of people travel back and forth every day, so there is constant traffic, transition, and opportunities for everything that crossing these borders implies. The city is also known for its hustlers, and we were warned by the hotel staff, our driver Aziz, and guide Omar to be very careful.

The morning after we arrived, before we bade farewell to Omar and Aziz, Omar led us through the souks of bright vegetables and luscious fruits, pale chickens hanging by their feet, mounds of red meats, crusty golden breads, multi-flavored olives, and more. Women from the Rif wearing their red-and-white-striped cloth skirts and embroidered wide-brimmed hats had come to sell their homemade cheeses. Aziz advised that the best is made from goat's milk, but theirs was a mixture of cow and sheep's milk. We passed by the historic American Legation, where during World War II much of the Allied landings into North Africa were planned, and later stopped at the Hotel Continental for a coffee. The old hotel gleams from the outside, but from the inside you can tell it's seen better days. It has been the home for many film crews shooting exotic movies. Photos of John Malkovich and Francis Ford Coppola hung in the antique shop next door.

Omar had been guiding us for several jam-packed days, but he was hopping a bus back to Fez to host a family wedding party. Aziz felt nervous about leaving us on our own, but we insisted that he take a few days off and pick us up later in the week. But before he would cut us loose, he drove us to a resort outside of Tangier where mansions abound, the coast is expansive with rolling sea, and the Grotto of Hercules is hidden underneath the baked earth.

Yes, Hercules lived here, and he is heralded by a festive "See Stone Mountain" feel in the square above his seaside cave home. Sea shells are attractively embedded in the stucco walls of turquoise buildings, and a giant mural of the brawny hero is painted on a rock wall. Camels are saddled and ready to ride. A small boy in costume with donkey in tow asked if we'd like to take a picture. Jim said no. I said yes. We paid him a small price and snapped. Traditionally dressed Muslim women gossiped on a terrace with the white-capped waves crashing below them.

As we walked down into the cave, the guide told us the story of Hercules and the Berbers who had lived there later. He pointed ahead to where the rock walls were splayed open in the shape of the African continent with the ocean lapping just beyond the massive crack. I was startled. A couple of months before—on Jim's birthday—I had dreamed of *this place*, not knowing what or where it was. In my dream, Jim and I were at an enormous cave with a vast body of water at the foot of the opening, which was also at a resort. Our daughter Bret had come across the water by herself in an inflatable boat, and I was completely impressed by this. She had come to tell us that no one could find my grandmother (who died last August). Bret and I would cross the sea again, but this time we would use a more substantial craft that I would drive. The next morning I recorded the dream, because I thought it so interesting, something I needed to contemplate. Finding it in Morocco as an ancient home for myths and legends and people who lived and breathed was surreal. Was it some sort of premonition? Why? What did it mean?

I told Aziz my weird tale as we drove us back to Tangier. He found a quay-side bistro where we inhaled a lunch of crispy fried squid, whole whiting, grilled shrimp, and rice. It was mouth-wateringly delicious and authentic—not a tourist spot—and some of the best fish we'd eaten anywhere. Then we wished Aziz a happy time off and walked to a well-known bookstore, which supposedly had a good selection of English volumes. But the only one we found was a Moroccan cookbook with recipes of many of the richly spiced dishes we'd been savoring. I bought it, thinking I would eventually have a Moroccan feast of a dinner party. But the store itself was dark and somewhat foreboding, and I didn't get the rush of excitement I usually get from bookstores.

That evening we had dinner in the hotel. Then we retreated to our room, where we sipped icy bourbon on our whitewashed terrace with its glorious view of the port of Tangier and the blue sea beyond. Tomorrow we would venture deeper into the city, but for the moment this was close enough.

CHAPTER THIRTY-EIGHT

Mission Accomplished

C LEAR LIGHT BURST open the sky, illuminating clues to Henri Matisse hidden in the muddle of Tangier. We stood on the periphery of the Grand Socco looking up and down for the way to the Grand Hotel Villa de France, where the Matisses had stayed and Henri had glimpsed scenes that matched his artistic vision. Jim was armed with a book of the paintings, and I carried my Morocco guide and map. We looked every bit the awkward rube tourists, but most Moroccans don't know much, if anything, about the artist whose lush paintings have etched the colors and forms of their country in the minds of art-lovers throughout the world. A couple of guides, real or faux, approached us, but we convincingly declined. I don't engage in conversation with hustlers unless it feels safe and right. In any case, we wanted to be on our own.

We were looking for the rue d'Angleterre and finally figured out that it was past the lovely English church of St. Andrews, with its wild and unruly secret garden of a cemetery whose earth contains the remains of journalist Walter Harris, members of the Royal Canadian Air Force, and other English-speaking expatriates who found magic in this enigmatic city. What allure or circumstance of life had drawn and kept them here? I didn't recognize their names or know their stories, but the mysterious unkempt graves were a summons to consider them. Time has taken its toll, the world here has changed. This yard must have been pristine once, and probably cared for by some of its now-eternal residents. The congregation is surely much diminished, which implies a lack of funds for upkeep. Any families of the dearly departed have likely moved on, and friends are themselves in the ground elsewhere. The earth is taking back her own. Nature has prevailed.

We wandered through the overrun and sun-dappled garden before walking up the street to the Matisses' hotel, which must have been quite grand in 1912 and 1913, when they were here, but now is shut and surrounded by its own jungle of neglect. Jim studied old pictures of the lodging and of the scenes Matisse painted, and finally pointed out the room where Monsieur and Madame must have stayed. It is always a thrill to make such discoveries, but for Jim it's even more satisfying to find the angle that intrigued Henri enough to color a canvas with his mental picture of it.

Our great goal for the day was in the Kasbah, and, miraculously, we found our way the first time we climbed the hill. We walked through the gate of Bab el-Assa, and Jim realized the exact perspective that was the subject of his favorite Matisse painting—"La Porte de la Casbah," from 1912-13—on the huge poster we had hanging at our apartment in Collioure. Jim sat down to sketch while I looked around. A Kasbah (most common spelling) is the walled citadel at the highest point of North African cities. This one had white and blue walls and stunning vistas of the sapphire sea beyond. Mansions framed one side of the wide courtyard with terraces and views beyond the ramparts. If I were a resident, this is the address I would want.

We diligently and sometimes luckily found all of Matisse's vistas. A couple of times we didn't notice the "eyescapes" as we walked in one direction on the narrow cobbled streets; but then when we came back from the other direction, we would have moments of *Aha! We've found the right scene!*

A friendly Belgian couple pointed out what they thought was the bar where the Rolling Stones used to hang out. I wasn't so sure, but okay, we went in and sat down. I still think it a usurper, but from there we gazed onto the rooftop terrace of the villa that the heiress Barbara Hutton owned for many years. The outdoor space and garden were inviting, though in need of a fluff-up. I could imagine the swell parties and glamorous guest lists Ms. Hutton must have engineered. Unlike M. Matisse, her name is well known here. She was a friend to Morocco's people (and animals) and endowed many good works. We also checked out her address from the street. Not bad, as the Hotel Saint Germain's M. Malric would say.

The only potentially smarmy experience we had was with a fairly neat and well-dressed guy who told us he'd take us to Paul Bowles' house. I was suspicious, but we were on a relatively spacious and clean street, so we went along. The street's name was accurate, but when the man started up a tight staircase, we said no thanks and left. Did he have good intentions? I don't know, but my radar was up, and there was no way I would've followed him at that point—especially since the "Rolling-Stones-hangout" owner had told the man we were his friends, which I interpreted as a message to leave us alone.

When we descended from this heavenly summit of Matisse Land, it was market day and the medina was filled with Riffian peasant women with their red-and-white skirts and broad straw hats. Their look and style is totally different than the women who are covered from head to toe in a loose caftan or djellaba, scarf, and veil. Due to Tangier's proximity to Spain and an area that is still Spanish Morocco, many people greeted each other with "ola" rather than "bonjour."

It was a wonderfully satisfying Matisse day, and we rewarded ourselves with cocktails in El Minzah's merely perfect bar before our last piquant dinner in the restaurant. Mission accomplished. We packed our bags.

* * *

THE NEXT MORNING we reunited with Aziz, who drove us back to Casablanca along the miles and miles of undeveloped coastline. This would be an unbelievable sight in the U.S. or France. It is good to know that such an unspoiled seashore still exists, though I'm sure it wouldn't if Morocco weren't so poor.

Our flight back to France wasn't until late, and so we rested for a few hours at the Royal D'Anfa Hotel. That evening Aziz picked us up and drove us to his house for a home-cooked Moroccan dinner. It was a generous invitation that we were delighted to accept.

Aziz's wife was out of town, so when we arrived, his mother and two sisters kindly welcomed us to their home. His children were darling, and they all treated us as honored guests or friends they'd known for years. Aziz was the only one of his family who spoke English, and we don't speak Arabic or Berber, so our communication with one another was through body language, sign language, our sensations of tasting and touching, seeing, hearing, and smelling, and the intimate messages that somehow one just feels or knows in his heart or gut.

Aziz's sister had graciously prepared our meal, which Aziz, Jim, and I were to eat before anyone else. What a feast—course after course of salads and chicken with olives and dishes whose names I can't remember (but which I totally devoured), and, for dessert, oranges as big as grapefruits, juicy and sweet.

After dinner, as we were putting on our coats to leave, the family offered us beautiful presents. Jim received a white hat that Aziz's father had brought home from his pilgrimage trip to Mecca, and I was given a sweet cedar box with a traditional silver necklace inside.

After we all hugged and kissed, Aziz drove us to the airport where we said our last goodbyes. In the blackness of night, the memory of that very special evening was a clear light illuminating our way back home.

(HAPTER THIRTY-NINE

Kicked Out... To Paris

LMOST AS SOON as we returned to Collioure from Morocco, our 67-year-old landlord informed us that we would have to move out of our garret loft so his latest girlfriend could move in. Even in the spirit of Sowing Late-ish Oats, I couldn't imagine why he would prefer a romantic arrangement to our good company and the enticing aromas of my cookery drifting down his stairwell (he dined with us quite often). But he did and kicked us out anyway.

As longtime homeowners and newish nomads, we weren't used to being evicted from our household. But in spite of that shock, this nudge gave us the opportunity to do something I had been wanting the three of us to do anyway—move to Paris!

In April 2004, Jim and I made a week-long trip to Paris to look for an apartment. The one we settled on was a beautiful flat right in the center of the city, in the 2nd Arrondissement next to the Place des Victoires. The Louvre was three blocks away, the Opera six. It was perfect!

Back in Collioure, we began packing up our possessions—our computers, books and files, Moroccan rugs and Haitian tin art, our Indian spreads, leather club chair and antique tables that I had hunted and gathered during the months we'd lived there. In June, we said tearful goodbyes to our new friends, put Snapp in the truck we had rented, and drove away for the next chapter of our adventure.

It was, I have to admit, revolting that we'd acquired so much *stuff* to make our first French apartment functional, comfortable, and reflective of us that we had to rent a truck to move. Here we go again! Is this just how we are? Can we not change? I know a few things about myself: I require order where I live, and I must have beauty surrounding me. That goes for Jim, too. A life without beauty is empty, boring, dull, and—well, beauty-less. I wasn't cut out to live a plain life in any sense. It would break my spirit and render me null and void.

As I write these words, it's been nine months since we moved to Paris. Our new apartment is small though lovely—classically Parisian with a Moroccan twist—and dates from 1620 (Napoleon Bonaparte is said to have once lived in our building). The colors of our walls are spectacular—the green of Mimosa leaves in spring, and a luscious luminous blue accented with jewel tones in shades of aubergine and ruby. The apartment is *tres* chic, and looks and feels like us—with two exceptions. We have a closet of a kitchen, which shoots my usual entertaining style to hell (though we've learned to manage). And we wish we had another room or two. Americans are used to space.

I've adjusted more easily than Jim (as throughout our trip in France). Change is harder on him than me. He misses his writing desk, his blue Chinese rug, his classic rattan chairs. He misses space, and also the outdoors. It would, I admit, be nice if we at least had a balcony. But we're coming up on our first spring here, and Jim is planning to get some window boxes and plant impatiens, just like we had in our back garden at home.

One thing neither of us misses is a car. We gladly gave up our leased auto in lieu of walking or taking the Metro—and, only rarely, a taxi.

Snapp instantly became a popular dog about town. We couldn't take him for a walk without being stopped on the street by numerous admirers. The French love dogs, and Snapp had such a gentlemanly presence. People instantly recognized his grand spirit, his *soigné*. One summer day, two Japanese women asked me to take their picture with him.

You may notice that I've referred to Snapp in the past tense here.

Almost six months ago, after our first summer here, Snapp became very ill. He was nearly 13 years old, and his kidneys were failing. It was a long, sad autumn—one I'll remember as marked by waterproof pads all over our floors, and Snapp's increasing dismay at his situation; he would sit for an hour with his face toward the wall. A month ago (on February 15, 2005), we had to have him put to sleep, which broke our hearts. We lost our dear boy, pal, and treasured member of our family.

But Blair and Bret were here for Christmas 2004, and we'd rented a car and all of us had gone to Alsace for a few days. Mr. Snappman had one last adventure in France with his family.

It is good we left Collioure. As glowing as it is, Collioure is a very small town. I loved it and the region—the Mediterranean and Pyrenees, the vineyards cascading down the hillsides, and the Catalonian people and their traditional dance, the *sardane*. But the town shuts down after the tourist season—which makes it more authentic, in a way, but it's also a little dispiriting, especially to a couple of outsiders. Frankly, I wanted the heartbeat of Paris and all the cultural opportunities that come with it. I knew I wanted to live here. I'm a city girl at heart, and it's a delight just to step out the door and walk down any street at all here. Beauty waits around every corner, appearing when you least expect it. People are sitting at sidewalk cafés drinking coffees or glasses of wine. Store windows are artfully arranged, and boulangeries are loaded with cases of croissants and meringues. Restaurants are waiting to be tried.

We're in the center of this city of light, making new friends, attending the opera, listening to jazz. Our neighborhood is divine! It's good to live here. We've started a new life, and I feel at home.

Now *Chasing Matisse* is finally out, and you can read Jim's lovely rendering of our big adventure—or, let's say, *his* version of our story! Please support your favorite bookstore and pick up a copy—or click on Amazon.com.

But however you follow us, I hope our journey will inspire you to chase your own dreams, whatever they may be. We'll be chasing ours.

EPILOGUE

JIM AND I ended up spending 10 glorious years in France, and there wasn't one minute in all those days, weeks, and years that I wasn't thrilled to be there. We drove up, down, and across the country. I read many books about French historical figures and loads of French history, and we spent time in every single region of France. With all of our travels, and since I'm a research-aholic, I eventually became more familiar with France as a whole than most French people. I took pride in my extensive knowledge. It was a joy to learn everything I learned.

Along the way we forged lifelong friendships and immersed ourselves in art. I became one of the early bloggers for *HuffingtonPost.com*, and in 2008 Arianna Huffington herself called to ask me to cover the night Barack Obama won the presidency for the first time. I was recruited to be one of the first bloggers for HuffPo's International Page. What fun it all was!

Paris was my home—Paris *is* my home. But that is a story for another day.

ACKNOWLEDGMENTS

THERE WERE SO many people who helped us on our magnificent journey chasing Matisse. When we arrived homeless in Paris, Michel Tessel, owner of French Home Rentals, gave us use of two apartments in which to stay for the first five weeks of our grand adventure. Not only that, he also introduced us to a fab Parisian dive restaurant that was (and I hope still is) a classic. Michel was a friend as well as a supporter.

Europe By Car gave us a deal on the station wagon that carried us and everything we owned on our trek across France. The fabulous Hotel St. Germain gave us a home in Paris before we moved there, and I will be ever grateful for the kindness of M. Malric—for his belief in us and our project—and for the hotel manager, Daniel, who was accommodating at every opportunity.

Our dear friend Alice Pennington-Mellor not only found us a house to live in in Brittany, she also introduced us to many wonderful people, including the lovely Anne Pierre-Humbert whose late husband's paintings we adored. Anne was our North Star in seeing how French artists lived and worked. We were fortunate to become part of her delightful circle of friends, which included Danièle Teisseire, Danièle's son, Luc, and her partner, Bertrand. Danièle's family had also been part of the Parisian art world. How lucky we were!

The same was true in Collioure, where we became friends with the ever-fabulous Monique Diderich, her husband, Bim, and Monique's friend Robert. This led to introductions to her gorgeous daughters

Joelle and Zoe. Joelle became one of my best friends in Paris. I miss that girl, but we're still very much in touch!

In Collioure we also met the dynamic Irish couple Gemma and Kevin O'Toole, who supported our verve with theirs. We solved world problems together on many occasions, and later spent time in Dublin with them seeing their city.

Back in Little Rock, our friends Susan and Ronnie May, Fritz and Connie Hollenberg, and Helen and Fred Harrison supported us and came to see us! Susan and Connie, along with Susan Gregory, were my Wise Women. Kathleen Hooker Jones and Maribeth Magby came over and packed boxes. Patti Kymer took care of an enormous range of details for us, before and after we left. What a debt we owed her, and she was the only one of our American buddies who visited us in every single place we lived in France! Sarah Herring was always there for us, as were our friends Thom Hall, Jerry Hooker, Greg Elliott, and J.O. Buckley. How does one ever express enough gratitude for true friendships?

I want to thank my late mother, Bobbye Arnold, who was willing to give Bret's cat, Cleo, and our dog, Snapp, a home when we left. She also stored the items that Blair and Bret thought they might want for easy access. This made Jim and me feel better—that the girls would have what they needed at their grandmother's house, where they happily thrived on many, many visits. That they would have their grandmother— or so we thought. I'll be ever sorry that she didn't live long enough to be spend some time chasing Matisse with us in France. She and my father, Bill Arnold, gave me my love of travel and my adventurous spirit. They opened the world to me. I was incredibly lucky to have them.

Elizabeth Cannon is a wonderful designer of women's couture. This was another lucky meeting when we came together in Paris. She also understood our journey and created the beautiful illustrations in this book. Elizabeth's talent speaks for itself, but I am in awe of it, and of her.

Editor Emeritus of *The Atlantic* William Whitworth has long been my friend and supporter. His belief in me and in my work honors me and makes me proud beyond words. I am ever grateful for his encouragement and nurturing.

I must thank all of our children. Jim's sons, David and Matt, were supportive of our journey, even as they were involved in their own adventures of marriage and starting families. We loved their visits to us in Europe.

My daughters, Blair and Bret, bore the brunt of our leaving, and they did it while understanding and encouraging us to follow our dream. Thank God Skype came into existence and we could talk every day and even see each other! Blair and Bret and Jim and I became even closer because of the distance between us. When we traveled to the U.S. to visit or they came to France, our time together was precious. We were together as much as possible and as our finances allowed.

And then there's my husband, Jim, who got the book contract that took us to France. He joined in my dream and went with it full force. How many men would do that? How many husbands love their wives this much? We were dreamers together, and we still are. Through the ups and downs of our challenges, we've kept on track and with each other. And he was my editor throughout writing my blog and turning it into this book. Hallelujah!

I'm sure there are names that should be here but aren't. Please forgive me if I've accidentally omitted you. Be sure that we loved and appreciated every tiny bit of support we got. We are ever grateful.

ABOUT BETH ARNOLD

A JOURNALIST AND award-winning writer who made her home in France from 2002 - 2012, Beth Arnold has written for such print venues as *Rolling Stone, GQ, InStyle, Self, American Way, Premiere,* and *Mirabella.* Online, besides her regular blogging for *The Huffington Post* and for www.betharnold.com (where she published her acclaimed "Letter From Paris"-branded column and podcasts), she has also written for *Salon.com, Vogue.com,* and *Marco Polo Quarterly,* among others. Her prime journalistic topics are culture, travel, art and design, politics, and people. She is interested in the sweet spot where art, design, and technology intersect with culture, and the boundaries we must set for ourselves in a digital world. She is fascinated by the evolution of our "selves" and the forces that have formed us.

Beth Arnold's work has been recognized by her peers, both in print and online. She was a finalist for a Bunting Fellowship at Radcliffe (for a novel) and a semi-finalist for a Nicholl Fellowship presented by the Academy of Motion Picture Arts and Sciences (for a screenplay). For one of her magazine articles, the Press Club of Dallas presented her with its prestigious Katie Award. In 2011, Arnold was named one of *Tripbase's* "100 Favourite Travel Writers," and her "Letter From Paris" was one of their Top 10 Paris Blogs of 2011.

Now, an exile returned from Paris but still a nomad at heart, she has been spending time with her family, rediscovering her own country, reckoning her spiritual path, and taking a 3 ½ month retreat by herself in India, which she calls "My Passage to India." This is a journey that she has not yet written about.